Researching and Writing in the Social Sciences

Christine A. Hult

Utah State University

Allyn and Bacon

Boston ✦ London ✦ Toronto ✦ Sydney ✦ Tokyo ✦ Singapore

Executive Editor: Joseph Opiela
Editorial Assistant: Susannah Davidson
Executive Marketing Manager: Lisa Kimball
Editorial-Production Administrator: Catherine Hetmansky
Editorial-Production Service: Ruttle, Shaw & Wetherill, Inc.
Composition Buyer: Linda Cox
Manufacturing Buyer: Aloka Rathnam
Cover Administrator: Suzanne Harbison

Library of Congress Cataloging-in-Publication Data
Hult, Christine A.
    Researching and writing in the social sciences/Christine A.
Hult.
        p.   cm.
    Includes bibliographical references and index.
    ISBN 0-205-16841-8
    1. Social Sciences—Research. 2. Social Sciences—Methodology.
I. Title.
H62.H725 1995
300'.72–dc20   95-23156
                                                                          CIP

Printed in the United States of America
10 9 8 7 6 5 4 3 2   00 99 98 97 96

Contents
+++

✦ **CHAPTER 5   Planning, Writing, and Revising Your Research Paper   113**

✦ **CHAPTER 6   Secondary Research Methods: Writing a Review Paper   137**

Preface

✦ ✦ ✦

Researching and Writing in the Social Sciences is an interdisciplinary research text that introduces you to research processes used in the social sciences (such as sociology and psychology). By reading this book you will gain experience in posing and solving problems common to an academic discipline, learning both primary research strategies and library research strategies. A comprehensive list of library resources is included to provide you with access to the important tools used by researchers.

Also included, as examples, are model student reports and research papers from disciplines in the social sciences to show you how your peers have solved research problems similar to your own. The exercises are designed to guide you through research processes and to teach the important supporting skills of summarizing, synthesizing, and critiquing source materials. Complete listings of citations show you how to document your sources within each discipline. In addition, this textbook stresses principles of research presentation and documentation common to the social sciences.

Many of the research guides now on the market fail to provide the comprehensive introduction to research that students need. Traditional research texts are often focused very narrowly on the library "term paper." They discuss formal considerations at length, from the form of notecards and bibliography cards to the form of a completed term paper. But they do not explore the entire research process, which is an integral part of any successful research project.

In contrast, *Researching and Writing in the Social Sciences* is a research text that explains and fosters intellectual inquiry, compares research in the various disciplines allied with the social sciences, and provides you with logical practice in research methodology.

Researching and Writing in the Social Sciences is divided into chapters of general information about research methods and resources in the academic disciplines and specific guidance in writing research papers for courses in the sciences and technology. You are first introduced to college research in general, and then to library resources (both general and discipline specific), library research methods, and primary research methods. Next, you receive explicit instruction in the planning, writing, and presentation of research papers in any field. Exercises throughout the book are designed to help you conduct your own research projects in a systematic and organized fashion.

Researching and Writing in the Social Sciences is both a comprehensive guide to research processes and an easy-to-use, complete reference tool designed to be used throughout your academic career and into your professional life. As with all research, my own work on this book has been a challenging process of discovery. I am grateful to the many researchers and theorists in the field of composition and rhetoric on whose work this book is built. Although I have cited in chapter notes only those authors whose ideas directly contributed to my own, many others contributed their ideas indirectly through journals, conferences, and textbooks. Teachers I have studied under and worked with, students who have patiently tried my ideas, and friends and family who have supported me along the way have all helped in the genesis of this book.

Finally, I am grateful to the editors and production team at Allyn & Bacon for their personal, professional attention, and to the reviewers of this edition of my manuscript.

1

✦ ✦ ✦

College Research

Researching, that is, exploring a problem systematically, is a crucial skill for an educated person. In college, you gain habits of mind that will serve you in every endeavor. Learning to research promotes careful, critical, systematic thinking. Learning to write promotes the effective communication of the ideas and insights gained in the research. Research and research writing necessarily go together, with each building on and promoting the other.

Research, broadly defined, is systematic inquiry designed to further our knowledge and understanding of a subject. Using this definition, nearly everything you do in college is "research." You seek to discover information about people, objects, and nature; to revise the information you discover in light of new information that comes to your attention; and to interpret your experience and communicate that interpretation to others through writing. This is how learning proceeds both for all of us as individuals and for human beings together as we search for knowledge and understanding of our world.

THE GENERAL PROCESS OF RESEARCH

Many accounts of the process of research have been written by scientists, artists, and philosophers. Researchers generally agree about the outlines of the process regardless of the discipline. The process often begins with a troubled feeling about something observed or experienced followed by a conscious probing for a solution to the problem, a time of subconscious activity, an intuition about the solution, and finally a systematic testing to verify the solution. This process may be described in a number of ways but may generally be divided into four stages: preparation, incubation, illumination, and verification.[1] These stages are discussed in order, but during a research project, each stage does not necessarily neatly follow the next. Quite probably the researcher moves back and forth freely among the stages and may even skip a stage for a time, but generally these four stages are present in most research projects.

Preparation

The preparation stage of the research process involves the first awareness in researchers that a problem or a question exists that needs systematic inquiry. Researchers formulate the problem and begin to explore it. As they attempt to articulate the exact dimensions and parameters of a particular problem, they use language or symbols of their discipline that can be more easily manipulated than unarticulated thoughts or the data itself. By stating the problem in a number of ways, looking at it from various angles, trying to define its distinctive characteristics, and attempting possible solutions, researchers come to define for themselves the subtleties of the problem. Preparation is generally systematic, but it may also include the researchers' prior experiences and the intuitions they have developed over time.

Incubation

The incubation stage usually follows the preparation stage and includes a period of intense subconscious activity that is hard to describe or define. Because it is so indistinct, people tend to discount it as unimportant, but the experience of many researchers shows that it is crucial to allow an idea to brew and simmer in the subconscious if a creative solution is to be reached. Perhaps you have had the experience of trying and failing to recall the name of a book you recently read. You tell your conversation partner, "Go ahead. It'll come to me." A few minutes later, when you are not consciously trying to recall the name but have gone on to other matters in your conversation, you announce, *"The Scarlet Letter,"* out of the blue. This is an example of the way your subconscious mind continues to work on a problem while your conscious mind has gone on to another activity.

We need to allow ourselves sufficient time for incubating. If you have ever watched a chicken egg in an incubator, you will have a sense of how this works. The egg rests in warmth and quiet; you see no action whatsoever, but you know that beneath that shell tremendous activity is going on. The first peck on the shell from the chick about to hatch comes as a surprise. This is analogous to the next stage of the process, illumination. You cannot really control the incubation of a problem, but you can prepare adequately and then give yourself enough time for subconscious activity.

Illumination

In the illumination stage, as with the hatching chick, there is an imaginative breakthrough. The idea begins to surface out of its concealing shell, perhaps a little at a time. Or the researcher leaps to a hypothesis, a possible solution to the problem, that seems intuitively to fit. Isaac Newton discovered the law of universal gravitation as he watched an apple fall, and Archimedes deduced his principle of the displacement of water while in the bathtub. The illumination of a hypothesis can come suddenly or gradually, after laborious effort or after an ordinary event that triggers the researcher's thinking along new lines. We must remember, though, that the hypothesis comes only after the researcher has investigated the problem thoroughly. The egg must be prepared, fertilized, warmed, and cared for. The solution to a complex problem will come only after much conscious study and preparation in conjunction with subconscious intuition. Sometimes the solution will not be so much a breakthrough as it will be a clearer understanding of the problem itself.

Verification

Once a researcher has arrived at a hypothesis, he or she must systematically test it to discern whether it adequately accounts for all occurrences. Sometimes, this testing requirement necessitates a formal laboratory research experiment; in other cases, only an informal check against the researcher's own experience is necessary. In the sciences, the verification stage tends to be highly rigorous, involved, and lengthy. One should also be prepared at the verification stage to discover that the original hypothesis will not work. Although we are often reluctant to make mistakes, without a willingness to err we would never be led to make an original contribution. Research often progresses as a series of increasingly intelligent mistakes through which the researcher ultimately is led to a reasonable and workable solution. Sometimes hypothesis testing goes on for years and, for a particularly promising hypothesis, is performed by the research community in general. To be judged as sound, or verified, such a hypothesis must survive the critical scrutiny of the whole research community.

A PHYSICIAN USES THE RESEARCH PROCESS

In the following essay, Charles Nicolle, a physician and scientist of the early twentieth century, describes the research process he used to discover the mechanism that transmitted the disease typhus.[2] As you read the essay, pay particular attention to the research process Nicolle outlines.

The Mechanism of the Transmission of Typhus

Charles Nicolle

It is in this way that the mode of transmission of exanthematic typhus was revealed to me. Take all those who for many years frequented the Moslem hospital of Tunis, I could daily observe typhus patients bedded next to patients suffering from the most diverse complaints. Like those before me, I was the daily and unhappy witness of the strange fact that this lack of segregation, although inexcusable in the case of so contagious a disease, was nevertheless not followed by infection. Those next to the bed of a typhus patient did not contract the disease, while, almost daily, during epidemic outbreaks, I would diagnose contagion in the *douars* (the Arab quarters of the town), and amongst hospital staff dealing with the reception of patients. Doctors and nurses became contaminated in the country in Tunis, but never in the hospital wards. One day, just like any other, immersed no doubt in the puzzle of the process of contagion in typhus, in any case not thinking of it consciously (of this I am quite sure), I entered the doors of the hospital, when a body at the bottom of the passage arrested my attention.

It was a customary spectacle to see poor natives, suffering from typhus, delirious and febrile as they were, gain the landing and collapse on the last steps. As always I strode over the prostrate body. It was at this very moment that the light struck me. When, a moment later, I entered the hospital, I had solved the problem. I knew beyond all possible doubt that this was it. This prostrate body and the door in front of which he had fallen, had suddenly shown me the barrier by which typhus had been arrested. For it to have been arrested, and, contagious as it was in entire regions of the country and in Tunis, for it to have remained harmless once the patient had passed the Reception Office, the agent of infection must have been arrested at this point. Now, what passed through this point? The patient had already been stripped of his clothing and of his underwear; he had been shaved and washed. It was therefore something outside himself, something that he carried on himself, in his underwear, or on his skin, which caused the infection. This could be nothing but a louse. Indeed, it was a louse. The fact that I had ignored this point, that all those who had been observing typhus from the beginnings of history (for it belongs to the most ancient ages of humanity) had failed to notice the incontrovertible and immediately fruitful solution of the method of transmission, had suddenly been revealed to me. I feel somewhat embarrassed about thus putting myself into the picture. If I do so, nevertheless it is because I believe what happened to me is a very edifying and clear example, such as I have failed to find in the case of others. I developed my observation with less timidity. At the time it still had many shortcomings. These, too, appear instructive to me.

If this solution had come home to me with an intuition so sharp that it was almost foreign to me, or at least to my mind, my reason nevertheless told me that it required an experimental demonstration.

Typhus is too serious a disease for experiments on human subjects. Fortunately, however, I knew of the sensitivity of monkeys. Experiments were therefore possible. Had this not been the case I should have published my discoveries without delay, since it was of such immediate benefit to everybody. However, because I could support the discovery with a demonstration, I guarded my secret for some weeks even from those close to me, and made the necessary attempts to verify it. This work neither excited nor surprised me, and was brought to its conclusion within two months.

In the course of this very brief period I experienced what many other discoverers must undoubtedly have experienced also, viz. strange sentiments of the pointlessness of any demonstration, of complete detachment of the mind, and of wearisome boredom. The evidence was so strong, that it was impossible for me to take any interest in the experiments. Had it been of no concern to anybody but myself, I well believe that I should not have pursued this course. It was because of vanity and self-love that I continued. Other thoughts occupied me as well. I confess a failing. It did not arrest my research work. The latter, as I have recounted, led easily and without a single day's delay to the confirmation of the truth, which I had known ever since that revealing event, of which I have spoken. ✦

Nicolle's struggle to discover a solution to the problem of typhus transmission illustrates a research process. Nicolle worked on the problem of typhus transmission both consciously and subconsciously; his "Eureka" experience came unexpectedly and forcefully. Nicolle was awarded the Nobel Prize for medicine in 1928 for his discovery and for the experiments that conclusively confirmed that typhus was indeed transmitted by parasites.

✦ QUESTIONS FOR DISCUSSION

1. What stages of the research process outlined in this chapter are revealed in Nicolle's description?
2. What incongruity led Nicolle to research the question of typhus transmission?
3. What experience triggered the solution to the problem?
4. What procedures did Nicolle use to verify his hypothesis?

5. You may have noticed that Nicolle grew bored at points during his research. What kept him going?

✦ EXERCISES

1. The four research stages discussed in this chapter come from words we often associate with different contexts. For example, we use the term *preparation* in connection with preparing dinner or preparing for a test. First, briefly describe a situation (other than research) commonly associated with each term. Then list any similarities between the connotation of each word in your situation and the particular research stage.

   A. To prepare:
   B. To incubate:
   C. To illuminate:
   D. To verify:

2. Think of an activity with which you are familiar, such as a sport (football or tennis), a hobby (cooking or gardening), or an art (painting or dancing). In one paragraph, describe the process you use when participating in the activity and relate the process to the research stages discussed in this chapter (preparation, incubation, illumination, and verification).

THE IMPORTANCE OF PREPARATION IN THE SOCIAL SCIENCES

The motivation or impetus for much social scientific research is an observed event or experience that challenges our existing ideas and promotes inquiry. In the context of existing theories, such an event is incongruous and thus sparks in the researcher's mind a question or problem to be investigated. The researcher must be prepared to recognize the inconsistency and see its importance. Therefore, he or she must be familiar with current theories and concepts in the field. In general, the aim of all social scientific work is to improve the relationship between our ideas (theories and concepts about the world) and our actual experiences (observations of the world). Social scientists who have created and tested a hypothesis must then report their findings to other scientists through publication. The goals of publishing one's findings include having others accept the hypothesis as sound and testable, communicating knowledge, and/or stimulating further research and discussion. The forums of social science—the professional organizations and societies, journals, universities, and research centers—combine to resolve social scientific issues to the benefit of all social scientists.

It is these forums of social science that necessitate writing. The best research in the world will be of no consequence if the social scientist is unable to communicate his or her results clearly to other social scientists through writing. Two major forms of writing done by social scientists are treated in this book: the *research report* (discussed in Chapter 4) and the *review paper* (discussed in Chapter 6).

THE IMPORTANCE OF FORMULATING AND TESTING HYPOTHESES

On the basis of a social scientist's prior knowledge and preparation, he or she formulates a hypothesis to account for the observed phenomenon that presents a problem. Arriving at a hypothesis takes much effort on the part of the researcher. Brainstorming for possible hypotheses is an important component of research, because the researcher can creatively make conjectures based on prior experience. The researcher may have to test several possible hypotheses before deciding which one seems to account for the observed phenomenon.

The following outline describes the systematic way that social scientists customarily proceed, often called the "scientific method":

1. The researcher formulates a question and develops a hypothesis that might shed light on the question posed.
2. On the basis of the hypothesis, the researcher predicts what should be observed under specified conditions and circumstances.
3. The researcher makes the necessary observations, generally using carefully designed, controlled experiments.
4. The researcher either accepts or rejects the hypothesis depending on whether or not the actual observations corresponded with the predicted observations.

THE INQUIRY PROCESS IN SOCIAL SCIENCE

Social sciences, such as psychology, anthropology, political science, sociology, economics, and education, have as their overall goal the systematic study of human behavior and human societies. The social sciences developed much later than the natural and physical sciences and so are comparatively young disciplines. Because social sciences followed the enormously successful and influential natural and physical sciences, they understandably adopted much of the scientific method—its goals, procedures, and standards. The field of sociology, for example, has been called the science of social organization; psychology has been called the science of the mind. Many social scientists today study people using the scientific method: they develop hypotheses and design and conduct controlled experiments to test those hypotheses.

A notorious example of a controlled social science experiment was conducted by Stanley Milgram, a Yale psychologist, during the 1960s.[3] Milgram sought to determine to what extent ordinary individuals would obey the orders of an authority figure. Through his experiment, he wished to probe the psychological processes that allowed the Germans to carry out mass human exterminations during World War II. Using simulated shock experiments, which were admittedly controversial, Milgram showed that an alarming proportion of adults (65 percent of those tested) were willing to inflict severe and, as far as they knew, permanent damage on strangers simply because they were instructed to do so by an authority figure, in this case the experimenter. The conclusions Milgram draws from this experiment are frightening:

> This is, perhaps, the most fundamental lesson of our study: ordinary people, simply doing their jobs, and without any particular hostility on their part, can become agents in a terrible destructive process. Moreover, even when the destructive effects of their work become patently clear, and they are asked to carry out actions incompatible with fundamental standards of morality, relatively few people have the resources needed to resist authority. A variety of inhibitions against disobeying authority come into play and successfully keep the person in his place.[4]

The research process used by Milgram closely follows that of other scientific research. His research began with a starting question: How could Hitler have succeeded in marshaling so much support from those who were called on to carry out his inhuman orders? After sufficient preparation, Milgram set out to determine the extent to which ordinary individuals would obey immoral orders. The psychologists were surprised by their results, which showed a large percentage of normal people obeying immoral orders from an authority figure. From the results, Milgram was able to verify that, indeed, there was something in human nature that could explain the behavior of so many Germans during World War II. The people who followed orders to annihilate others were not brutal, sadistic monsters, he stated, but rather normal people who acted out of a sense of duty and obligation to their country and their leader.

THE IMPORTANCE OF
OBSERVING HUMAN BEHAVIOR

A great number of the experiments created by social scientists are designed to observe human behavior. Because the goal of any science is the systematic, objective study of phenomena, the social sciences had to observe those aspects of humans that were observable. The only objectively observable part of humanity is behavior. We cannot observe human emotions or consciousness directly, but we can observe the behavior that results from feelings and thoughts in human consciousness. The social sciences, consequently, have focused heavily on behavior and thus have been called the behavioral sciences. The Milgram experiment is an example of a behavioral-science experiment. Milgram observed how his subjects behaved in a carefully controlled experimental setting to arrive at his conclusions about why people act as they do.

THE IMPORTANCE OF UNDERSTANDING
HUMAN CONSCIOUSNESS

Many people, both within and outside the social sciences, have felt that this objectification of observable human behavior produces a false picture of human beings. The real "inside" of a person may be missed when only the behavior manifested on the outside is observed. Human beings are conscious beings; we have thoughts, feelings, and intuitions that are private and never seen by others. Some in the social sciences argue that because we cannot observe consciousness directly, it is not a proper subject for scientific study at all. Others take the position that it is not only appropriate to study human consciousness but also essential, because consciousness is what makes us uniquely human. Modern social scientists have developed methods of exploring human consciousness that are admittedly subjective but nevertheless reveal important information about how people think and feel. Such methods include case studies of individuals, clinical evaluation, psychoanalysis, and hypnosis.

Social scientists also study the interaction among people in societies. A social scientist attempting to discover social rules and conventions is somewhat analogous to a natural scientist attempting to discover laws of nature. The social rules and conventions adopted by a particular society are important for understanding human behavior within that society. For example, a Polynesian native accustomed to using shells as money would have a rude awakening in an American marketplace where, by convention, slips of paper are used to trade for goods and services. The slip of paper we accept as a dollar bill has meaning for us only within our particular set of social conventions. Much of the work done in social sciences attempts to describe and define the social laws, rules, and conventions by which people operate within societies.

An example of a social scientist whose work has been important in the twentieth century is the Austrian psychologist Sigmund Freud, who sought to describe and predict the complex operation of the human subconscious mind. Freud also sought to apply his theories of individuals to the operation of human beings in societies. In one of his last books, *Civilization and Its Discontents,* he expressed his views on the broad question of the human being's place in the world.[5] Freud posed the question, Why is it hard for humankind to be happy in civilization? Through his years of preparation and study, Freud was able to posit the hypothesis that unhappiness is due to the inevitable conflict between the demands of instincts (aggression and ego gratification) and the restrictions of civilized society:

> If civilization imposes such great sacrifices not only on man's sexuality but on his aggressivity, we can understand better why it is hard for him to be happy in that civilization. In fact, primitive man was better off in knowing no restrictions of instinct. To counterbalance this, his prospects of enjoying this happiness for any length of time were very slender. Civilized man has exchanged a portion of his possibilities of happiness for a portion of security.[6]

Freud's sociological theories have been as influential as his psychological theories. Verification of this particular hypothesis—that instinct and society conflict—was achieved through Freud's extensive citation of examples taken from psychological case studies and from primitive and modern societies (including the Soviet Union and the United States). Through these examples, Freud showed that human instincts are in conflict with society's constraints.

As discussed at the opening of this section on the social sciences, researchers attempt to describe and predict human behavior and human relationships in society. Barzun and Graff, in their text *The Modern Researcher,* observe that "the works of social science that have made the strongest mark on the modern mind have been those that combined description with enumeration and imparted the results with imaginative power."[7] The work of Freud is a classic example of the way good social science research combines an understanding of individual human behavior and consciousness with an understanding of how people are organized and influenced by the societies in which they live and operate.

OBJECTIVITY VERSUS SUBJECTIVITY

In the sciences, researchers attempt to remove their own particular preferences, desires, and hopes from the experimental process as much as possible. Scientific researchers are looking for "objective" truth. However, because each researcher as observer necessarily brings background preparation, knowledge, and experience to the situation, it is seldom possible to remove the researcher from the research altogether. But what about the social sciences? Can they be as objective as the natural sciences in their search for knowledge and understanding? Many would charge that subjectivity and values are inescapable and necessary parts of social science research. The social scientist studies people, social systems, and social conventions. As a person, the researcher is necessarily a part of the system being studied. Perhaps this is not altogether a bad thing. A social scientist's own beliefs, attitudes, and values can contribute to his or her understanding of what is being observed, even though he or she can, to a certain degree, demonstrate detachment from a situation and function as a relatively impartial observer. But the question of objectivity and subjectivity in the social sciences is not easily resolved, because it is not always possible to know exactly what subjective influences are affecting "objective" research. The issue of subjectivity versus objectivity is the cause of much ferment and continual debate within the social science fields as these young disciplines seek to define for themselves an appropriate method, whether it is modeled after the scientific method or something quite different.

✦ **QUESTIONS FOR DISCUSSION**

1. What is the general goal of inquiry in the social sciences?
2. Why are social sciences often called "behavioral sciences"?
3. What is meant by the understanding of human consciousness?
4. What is the relationship between objectivity and subjectivity in the social sciences?

NOTES

1. Adaptation of excerpt from "The Four Stages of Inquiry," in Richard E. Young, Alton L. Becker, and Kenneth L. Pike, *Rhetoric: Discovery and Change* (New York: Harcourt Brace Jovanovich, Inc., 1970). Reprinted by permission of the publisher. This four-step problem-solving process (preparation, incubation, illumination, verification) was first outlined by Wallas in 1926 (*The Art of Thought*, New York: Harcourt, Brace).

2. Charles Nicolle, "The Mechanism and Transmission of Typhus," in Rene Taton, *Reason and Chance in Scientific Discovery* (New York: Philosophical Library, 1957), pp. 76–78. Reprinted by permission of Philosophical Library, Inc.

3. Stanley Milgram, *Obedience to Authority: An Experimental View* (New York: Harper & Row, 1974).

4. Milgram, p. 6.

5. Sigmund Freud, *Civilization and Its Discontents*, edited and translated by James Strachey (New York: W. W. Norton, 1961).

6. Freud, p. 62.

7. Jacques Barzun and Henry F. Graff, *The Modern Researcher*, rev. ed. (New York: Harcourt Brace and World, 1970), p. 245.

2

✦ ✦ ✦

Library Resources

Students' experience researching in libraries varies from expert to novice. Your own experience will fall somewhere along that continuum. But even if you have used libraries before, there is always more to learn. College libraries are typically large, complex entities that often seem to have a life of their own. They are constantly changing as new information and methods to access information are incorporated by librarians.

Your library contains many important general research tools with which you need to become familiar to conduct any research project. Also in your library are specific resources that are important for research in particular disciplines. This chapter covers information on library resources in the social sciences. You may find that some of this chapter is review, but you will certainly also encounter sources of which you were not previously aware.

THE LIBRARY REFERENCE AREA

Most library research begins in the library reference area. Reference librarians are excellent resources when you need help finding information in the library. However, you need to know enough about libraries to ask the librarian to help you, just as you need to know enough about your car to suggest to a mechanic where to begin when your car needs repair. It is not productive to walk up to a mechanic and simply ask for help. You need to explain the specifics of your particular problem and describe the make, model, age, and condition of your car. Similarly, you need to tell a librarian what kind of project you are working on, what information you need, and in what form that information is likely to be stored. So that you can ask the right questions, you must first take the time to learn your way around the library. Working your way through this chapter is a good place to begin. Librarians use terminology that you should become familiar with. Particular terms are defined throughout this chapter. We will start by looking at some major library sources and what distinguishes them.

In the heading of this section of the chapter you saw the word *reference*. As you might suspect, a reference is something that *refers* to something else. In your library there is an area designated as the reference area and a person called the reference librarian. The reference area may be a separate room or simply a section of the library. In the reference area you will find books containing brief factual answers to such questions as, What is the meaning of a particular word? What is the population density of a particular state? What is the birthplace of a certain famous person? Also in the reference area are books that refer you to other sources. These library tools—bibliographies and indexes—will help you find particular articles written about particular subjects. The reference area of the library is usually the place to begin any research project. Reference sources include the following general types of works:

Abstracts: Short summaries of larger works; may be included in an index

Almanacs: Compendia of useful and interesting facts on specific subjects

Atlases: Bound volumes of maps, charts, or tables illustrating a specific subject

Bibliographies: Lists of books or articles about particular related subjects

Biographies: Works that provide information on the life and writings of famous people, living and dead

Dictionaries: Works that provide information about words, such as meaning, spelling, usage, pronunciation

Encyclopedias: Works that provide concise overviews of topics, including people, places, ideas, subject areas

Handbooks: Books of instruction, guidance, or information of a general nature

Indexes: Books or parts of books that point to where information can be found, such as in journals, magazines, newspapers, or books

Reviews: Works that analyze and comment on other works, such as films, novels, plays, or even research

Serials: Periodicals (magazines) that are published at specific intervals and professional (scholarly) journals that contain articles and research reports in a specific field

ONLINE COMPUTER CATALOGS

One of the most visible computer tools in libraries today is the online catalog. Such a system, which supplements or replaces the traditional card catalog, is designed to provide library materials service, such as circulation, cataloging, and location of materials within the library collection. Most online catalogs are searchable by author, title, and subject (as are card catalogs), but many are also searchable by keyword or by combinations of subjects or keywords.

You should become familiar with your library's online catalog as soon as possible. (Note: Some online catalogs cover only the most recent additions to the library's collection, in which case older books still may be found by looking in the card catalog.) Check with your librarian to find out exactly what materials (e.g., books, magazines, journals, government documents) are cataloged in your library's online catalog.

How to Search the Online Catalog

When you log-on to your library's online catalog, you will typically see a menu of choices listing the various databases available for searching. For example, the library at my university includes the following databases in its online catalog, all searchable from the same computer. To enter any one of these databases, you make the appropriate selection from the main menu.

General Book Collection (OPAC, Online Public Access Catalog) lists the books, government documents, and audiovisual materials in the library.

General Periodicals Index (WRGA, Wilson Readers' Guide to Periodical Literature) lists articles from popular magazines and journals and corresponds to the *Readers' Guide to Periodical Literature* from 1985 to the present.

To search for articles written in particular disciplines, our library also provides several specialized databases in the online catalog:

Wilson Guide to Business Periodicals, Education Index, and the Social Sciences Index (WSOC) indexes journal articles in business, education, and social sciences.

Wilson Guide to Art Index and Humanities Index (WHUM) indexes journal articles in humanities and arts.

Wilson Guide to Applied Science and Technology Index, Biological and Agricultural Sciences Index, and General Sciences Index (WSCI) indexes journal articles in sciences, agriculture, and technology.

Current Contents Articles and Journals (CART and CJOU) indexes the table of contents for recent journal issues in several fields of the sciences and social sciences (Figure 2-1).

```
                    WELCOME
            UTAH STATE UNIVERSITY
               MERRILL LIBRARY

To select a database, type appropriate four letter
code, i.e. OPAC and press ENTER. To return to this
menu screen, type START.

              MERLIN
OPAC      USU LIBRARY COLLECTION
          JOURNAL/PERIODICAL INDEXES
*WRGA     POPULAR MAGAZINE INDEX
*WHUM     HUMANITIES & ART INDEXES
*WSCI     AGRICULTURE/BIOLOGY & SCIENCE
          TECHNOLOGY
*WSOC     BUSINESS/EDUCATION & SOCIAL SCIENCES
          CURRENT CONTENTS
*CART     CURRENT CONTENTS ARTICLES
*CJOU     CURRENT CONTENTS JOURNALS
          * Databases that require Sign-On.
--------------------Page 1 of 1------------------
HELP    Select a database label from above
        NEWs (Library System News)

Database Selection:
Alt-Z FOR HELP3 VT100    3 FDX 3 19200 N81 3 LOG
CLOSED 3 PRINT OFF 3 OFF-LINE
```

FIGURE 2-1   Main Menu

You will need to know enough about how information in your library is organized to be able to select the appropriate databases from the computer menu. Many libraries offer instruction in the use of their online catalog. If yours does not, plan to spend the time you need to become a confident user of your library's computer system. Take advantage of online help menus provided by the computer, and be sure to ask a librarian for help when stumped. Librarians are trained to be "user friendly."

Internet

Many libraries provide access to information in other libraries through Internet services via computer. The Internet is a computer "network of networks" from campuses as well as regional, national, and even international sources that are joined into a single network. It is like a worldwide network of information highways with all the freeways and byways connected. Internet in our library offers an opportunity to explore other Utah library catalogs, for example, or to find information through many different lists or "gophers" that store information. Students can use Internet to find information on sample job interview questions offered in a gopher by USU's career services. Or, you can locate the most recent White House press release on the budget.

The main challenge right now is learning how to "mine" the Internet, to tap into its vast array of information. New systems to help consumers find their way through the maze on the information superhighway are constantly being developed. There are, for example, online services such as America Online that provide easy-to-use interfaces, allowing access to hundreds of resources. There are also navigational helpers such as the World Wide Web, which have established standards and protocols to make searching among a variety of networks virtually seamless.

Two popular interfaces to information on the Internet are Mosaic and Netscape. Mosaic was developed by the National Center for Supercomputing Applications (NCSA) in Champaign, Illinois. The Mosaic and Netscape client/server applications are designed so that information can be distributed and retrieved over the Internet using a graphical user interface, thus making it possible for clients to locate other servers of different types along the Internet while maintaining the same consistent graphics on the client's screen. Through hypertext links, users can move easily about the Internet by simply pointing and clicking on Mosaic or Netscape graphics. The Internet is in constant flux and growing at a phenomenal rate, so you would be wise to explore the Internet resources available on your particular campus. The best way to learn about Internet is to practice using it yourself.

Subject Headings

When using online catalogs, it is important to become familiar with the *Library of Congress Subject Headings (LCSH)*, a listing of subject areas using specific terminology. To search the database by subject, you must provide the computer with exact subject headings, those officially used by the Library of Congress as listed in the *LCSH*. However, sometimes it is difficult to predict which terms will be used. The *LCSH* is your key or guide to the subjects recognized by the online catalog: it lists the subject headings that are assigned to books and materials in the library's collection. As there is often more than one way to describe a topic, the *LCSH* gives the exact format (wording and punctuation) for subject headings as they will appear in the database.

Before beginning to search the online catalog, first check the *LCSH* to become familiar with all the possible subject terms related to your topic. Keep a comprehensive list of all the subject headings that you are using in your search of the library's holdings. These subject headings will be useful to you not only for the library's book collection, but also when you begin searching for articles in magazines and journals.

Title and Author Searches

The computer can search quickly through its database when you provide it with a correct title or an author's name (T = Title; A = Author). If there is more than one work by an author, the computer lists them all, and then allows you to select the one you are looking for. You may need to request an expanded screen (or "long view") with more details about the specific work you have selected. The computer should also let you know whether or not the book has been checked out of the library and provide you with a call number to help you locate the book. In some libraries, it is possible to place a "hold" on a work through the computer, with a provision that you will be notified as soon as the book is back in circulation.

Subject Searches

To search by subject, once again be certain to use the exact *LCSH* subject heading as found in the *LCSH* volumes. Tell the computer that you intend to search by subject by entering the appropriate command along with the exact subject heading (in our library, for example, you type "S = Subject"). The computer then tells you how many items in its database are cataloged under that subject heading (called the number of "hits") and provides you with a list of titles (Figure 2-2).

```
Search Request: S=ACUPUNCTURE                        USU CATALOG
BOOK - Record 1 of 8 Entries Found                     Long View
----------------------------------------------------------------
Author:            Stux, Gabriel.

Title:             Basics of acupuncture
Published:         Berlin ; New York : Springer-Verlag, c1988.
Description:       xi, 272 p. : ill. ; 19 cm.

Subjects:          Acupuncture.

Other authors:     Pomeranz, Bruce, 1937-

Notes:             Includes index.
                   Bibliography: p. 253-257.

-----------------    + Page 1 of 2   ------------------------
STArt over           BRIef view         <F8> FORward page
HELp                 INDex              <F6> NEXt record
OTHer options
```

```
Search Request: S=ACUPUNCTURE                        USU CATALOG
BOOK - Record 1 of 8 Entries Found                     Long View
----------------------------------------------------------------
Title:             Basics of acupuncture
----------------------------------------------------------------
LOCATION:          CALL NUMBER:        STATUS:
SciTech LIBRARY    RM184.S79 1988      Not checked out
STACKS-4TH FLOOR

-----------------    + Page 2 of 2   ------------------------
STArt over           BRIef view         <F7>  BACk page
HELp                 INDex              <F6> NEXt record
OTHer options

NEXT COMMAND:
Alt-Z FOR HELP3 VT100    3 FDX 3 19200 N81 3 LOG CLOSED 3
PRINT OFF 3 OFF-LINE
```

FIGURE 2-2   Online Subject Search

If the computer tells you that there are several hundred books with your subject heading, you may need to narrow your subject search. The *LCSH* will provide you with narrower terms (labeled "NT"). Or you can narrow your search by combining key words (see Keyword Searching section in this chapter). On the other hand, if the computer tells you there are only one or two titles with your subject heading, you may need to broaden your subject search. Again, the *LCSH* will suggest related terms (labeled "RT") or broader terms ("BT") that you can try as well.

Call Number Searching

This is an excellent way to locate materials similar to works for which you currently have a call number. By typing in the exact call number of a known work, you can ask the computer to list all of the call numbers that come before and after that work in the computer's memory. This means that it is possible to read titles on the computer screen by call number, just as you would browse a shelf in the library and retrieve other books found on surrounding shelves.

Keyword Searching

Keyword searching allows for searching under the most important term or terms for your research project that you have identified. The computer locates items in its database that use a particular keyword anywhere in a work's record. However, if the record doesn't happen to include that particular keyword or term, the computer typically will not be able to supply the synonym. Therefore, you still need to try as many keywords and subject headings as you can think of in a database search. For example, if you are searching the subject UFOs, you might use "UFO" as a keyword. But you might also want to try other keywords, such as "flying saucers" or "paranormal events."

Advanced Keyword Searching

Using keywords, it is possible to perform combined searches of two or more terms. Combining keywords helps to limit an otherwise broad topic. For example, if you were interested in teenage pregnancy but only for the state of California, you could combine the terms "teenage pregnancy" and "California" to narrow your search, thus searching the collection only for those sources that include both keywords. This kind of focused searching offers distinct advantages over using a card catalog. If your library offers instruction in advanced database searching, you would be wise to take the opportunity to learn the "tricks of the trade" (Figure 2-3).

Recording Bibliographic Information

Once you have a listing of books from the online catalog, you need to note each book's specific call number so that you can locate it in your library's collection. It may be possible for you to send a print command from your online catalog to request a printout of your search results. If not, you will need to be certain you write down the titles, along with their complete bibliographic information, on your working bibliography in your research notebook. Complete bibliographic information includes:

```
Search Request: K=ACUPUNCTURE + CHINESE      USU CATALOG
BOOK - Record 1 of 1 Entry Found                Long View

Author:          Chuang, Yu-Min.

Title:           Chinese acupuncture : standard practices,
                 locations, illustrations / by Yu-min Chuang
                 (Yu-ming Chong).

Published:       Hanover, N. H. : Oriental Society, 1973.
Description:     98 p. : ill. ; 22 cm.

Subjects:        Acupuncture.

Notes:           English and Chinese.
-------------------------------------------------------------
LOCATION:          CALL NUMBER:     STATUS:
SciTech LIBRARY    RM184 .C58x      Not checked out
STACKS-4TH FLOOR
------------------  Page 1 of 1   ----------------------
STArt over         BRIef view
HELp
OTHer options

NEXT COMMAND:
Alt-Z FOR HELP3 VT100    3 FDX 3 19200 N81 3 LOG CLOSED 3
PRINT OFF 3 OFF-LINE
```

FIGURE 2-3   Online Keyword Search

Author(s) full name, including initials
Title of the book, including subtitles and editions
Place (city and state) where the book was published
Name of the book's publisher
Date of publication

MICROFORMS

A few libraries organize their holdings on microforms rather than computer databases or catalog cards. Microforms are either micro-film or microfiche; both make use of methods to condense information in a very compact form. Machines called microform readers are necessary to read either form. Information stored on microform is similar to that found on traditional cards. If your library uses this system, check with the reference librarian for instructions about using the microform readers.

LOCATING ARTICLES IN SERIALS: POPULAR PERIODICALS

Periodicals are popular magazines and newspapers printed at regular intervals, such as daily, weekly, monthly, or quarterly. It is possible to search for magazines and journals through both online computer searching and print indexes. The reference section of your library contains several indexes to articles found in periodicals. Two important indexes of general-interest periodicals are:

Magazine Index. Los Altos, CA.: Information Access, 1978 to present.
Readers' Guide to Periodical Literature. New York: Wilson, 1901 to present.

Both sources index articles in popular magazines. The *Readers' Guide* is available in chronologically bound volumes; each contains an alphabetical listing of articles from a particular year. (The current issues are paperbound.) The *Magazine Index* is available on microform and online computer systems. This index is extremely useful for very current topics, because it indexes about twice as many articles as the *Readers' Guide.* In both sources, entries are arranged both by subject and author. These indexes may also be available in your library in a computer database.

Newspapers

Your library probably stores back issues of newspapers on microform. To gain access to articles in the *New York Times,* use the *New York Times Index,* which lists all major articles from the *Times* from 1913 to the present. The *Newspaper Index* lists articles from the *Chicago Tribune, Los Angeles Times, New Orleans Times-Picayune,* and *Washington Post.* Both indexes are arranged by subject. For business news, use the *Wall Street Journal Index.* Newspaper indexes may be available in your library in both print and database forms.

Your library has a particular system for listing magazine and newspaper holdings. This serials listing may appear in the online catalog, in a separate catalog, in the main card catalog, on computer printouts, or on microform. Consult your librarian to determine which system your library uses. The serials listing tells you to which periodicals your library subscribes, where they are located in the library, the inclusive dates of the issues your library has, and whether the issues are in bound or unbound volumes or on microform.

Once you have obtained the call number of the magazine containing your article from the serials listing, you will be able to find the magazine itself, whether it is in a bound volume, in the current-periodicals section of the library, or on microform. Once you have the article in hand, be sure to copy down the complete publication information, which is often only abbreviated in the index. Writing everything down at this point will prevent your having to return to the library later for information you neglected to note originally.

Evaluating Periodicals

If you find the title of a magazine but are unsure of its nature or scope, a useful evaluative tool is *Katz's Magazines for Libraries*, 5th ed. (New York: Bowker, 1986). This work describes and explains magazines. Katz's guide can give you some insight into the magazine's purpose, reputation, and scope.

LOCATING ARTICLES IN SERIALS: PROFESSIONAL JOURNALS

When you are researching a technical subject, you want to refer to articles written on the subject by professionals in the field (Figure 2-4 on page 24). Professional journal articles, sometimes called serials because they are printed in series, are indexed in much the same way as the general periodicals previously discussed. However, numerous specialized indexes and databases exist for professional articles, and each index or database covers a particular discipline or subject area. (See "Discipline-Specific Resources" on page 28.)

Once you have located an appropriate index, begin looking up your topic in the most recent volume first. If you were researching the topic "drug abuse," Figure 2-5 on page 25 provides an example of what you might find in the *Social Sciences Index*.

For articles that sound promising for your research, copy down the complete citation. To find the full version of abbreviated journal names, turn to "Abbreviations of Periodicals Indexed," usually at the front of the index volume. For example, you would find that *Congr Q Wkly Rep* is the abbreviation for *Congressional Quarterly Weekly Reports*. Then locate the particular journal by using your library's listing of serial holdings, just as you did for magazines and newspapers. Professional journals are stored in bound or unbound volumes (the latter for very recent editions) or on microform. The citation you have obtained from the index is your key to finding a particular article. Thus, it is crucial that you copy down the citation information accurately and completely.

Many of the indexes to scholarly journals follow the format of the *Social Sciences Index* (see Figure 2-5). However, there are sometimes

```
Search Request:K=FAMILY AND COUNSELING BUSINESS/EDUCATION & SOC
WILSON Record -- 2 of 18 Entries Found                Long View
------------------------------------------------------------------
AUTHOR:        Aronen, Eeva.

TITLE:         The effect of family counselling on the mental
               health on 10-11-year-old children in low- and
               high risk families: a longitudinal approach.

SOURCE:        The Journal of Child Psychology and Psychiatry
               and Allied Disciplines 34:155-65 Feb  '93

SPECIAL FEATURES:
               bibl.

SUBJECT DESCRIPTORS:
               School children--Mental health.
               Mental illness--Prevention.
               Family counseling.
------------------------- Page 1 of 1 --------------------
STArt over          HOLdings              <F6> NEXt record
HELp                BRIef view            <F5> PREvious record
OTHer options       INDex
Held by library--type HOL for holdings information.
NEXT COMMAND:
Alt-Z FOR HELP3 VT100   3 FDX 3 19200 N81 3 LOG CLOSED 3 PRINT
OFF 3 OFF-LINE
```

FIGURE 2-4   Long View Journal Article

variations in the index formats. Take the time to get acquainted with the arrangement of each index by reading the explanation in the index's preface. If you are still confused about how an index is organized, ask your reference librarian for help. As mentioned before, many indexes are now contained on databases so that they may be searched with computers. Check with your librarian to discover which indexes in your library may be searched on computer.

LOCATING GOVERNMENT DOCUMENTS

The U.S. government is one of the largest publishers of information and is a rich source of materials in almost every field, from aeronautics to zoology. Government documents are sometimes listed in a separate database or catalog from the main online or card catalog. Check with your reference librarian to discern how your library catalogs its documents.

Dual career couples *See* Dual career families
Dual career families
　　See also
　　Commuter marriage
　　Work and family
　　Division of household labor and child care in dual-earner
　　African-American families with infants. Z. Hossain
　　and J. L. Roopnarine. bibl *Sex Roles* v29 p571-83 N '93
　　The division of household labor and wives' happiness:
　　ideology, employment, and perceptions of support.
　　D. L. Piña and V. L. Bengtson. bibl *J Marriage
　　Fam Rev* v55 p901-12 N '93
　　The dual-career commuter family: a lifestyle on the
　　move. E. A. Anderson and J. W. Spruill. bibl *Marriage
　　Fam Rev* v19 no1-2 p131-47 '93
　　Dual-earner couples in Singapore: an examination of
　　work and nonwork sources of their experienced burnout.
　　S. Aryee. bibl *Hum Relat* v46 p1441-68 D '93
　　Female employment and first union dissolution in Puerto
　　Rico. K. P. Carver and J. D. Teachman. bibl *J Marriage
　　Fam* v55 p686-98 Ag '93
Dual career marriage *See* Dual career families

FIGURE 2-5　Social Sciences Index

The *Monthly Catalog of United States Government Publications* is the
comprehensive bibliography that lists all publications received by the
Government Printing Office for printing and distribution. The *Monthly
Catalog*, established in 1895, is the best overall guide to finding government sources. At the back of each monthly register are indexes that provide access to the documents by authors, subjects, and series/report
numbers. The monthly indexes are cumulated (that is, brought together
into one volume) both semiannually and annually for ease of access.

Other ways to find government documents include the following
indexes:

Index to U.S. Government Periodicals
Public Affairs Information Services (PAIS)
Resources in Education (RIE)
U.S. Government Reports, Announcements and Index
(NTIS—National Technical Information Service)

The *Index to U.S. Government Periodicals* provides access by author and
subject to 180 government periodicals. The *PAIS* lists by subject current books, pamphlets, periodical articles, and government publications in the field of economics and public affairs. *RIE* lists government-
sponsored reports related to the field of education. The *U.S. Government
Reports, Announcements and Index (NTIS)* lists government-sponsored

research in the technical sciences by subject fields: aeronautics; agriculture; astronomy and astrophysics; atmospheric sciences; behavioral and social sciences; biological and medical sciences; chemistry; earth science and oceanography; electronic and electrical engineering; energy conversion; materials; mathematical sciences; mechanical, industrial, civil, and marine engineering; methods and equipment; military science; navigation, communications, detection; nuclear science and technology; physics; and propulsion and fuels.

OTHER TECHNOLOGIES

Online Database Services

To supplement the searches you have been able to conduct in your own library, online database searches may be conducted for you by trained search librarians who have access through a telecommunication link to a central databasing service such as DIALOG. When you want to conduct such a search, make an appointment with a librarian to discuss your search needs, possible databases, and likely subject headings. The librarian then conducts the search and provides you with a printout of sources or abstracts. The cost of the search is typically passed on to you, so you should discuss any search with a trained librarian first to decide whether it is feasible and economical. (See Figure 2-6.)

CD-ROM Searching

Many libraries are now providing patrons with the opportunity to search databases themselves, using microcomputers connected to compact disk units (CD-ROMs). With compact disk technology, large databases can be made accessible and easy to use. For example, the education index ERIC (Education Research Information Clearinghouse) is now available in this format, as is the business index ABI-INFORM. Check your library reference area to see whether such tools are available to you. These databases are subject specific, so you need to find out just which journals or subjects they index. But they often can provide a quick alternative to searching the print indexes on your subject. Another bonus of using CD-ROMs is that the information found in your search can usually be sent to a printer or downloaded onto your own computer disk.

As with any computerized search, it is important to know your subject headings and terminology. Many of the computer databases use their own "controlled vocabulary," which may vary slightly from the subject headings listed in the *LCSH*. Check with your librarian to discern whether there is a "thesaurus" or listing of subject headings for the

PRINTS User:U0020650 28Sep84 PRINT 13/5/1-117

Database— service date DIALOG File 1: ERIC - 66-84/Sep

EJ299865 HE518071
Many Colleges Limit Students' Use of Central Computers for Writing.
Turner, Judith Axler
CAUSE/EFFECT, v7 n3 p6-7 May 1984
Available from: UMI
Language: English
Document Type: POSITION PAPER (120); PROJECT DESCRIPTION (141)
Journal Announcement: CIJSEP84
Allocating limited resources to an unlimited demand is an issue faced by data processing management in higher education. Use of the central computer for word processing is creating a demand at many institutions that is stretching and exceeding the available computing resources. (Author/MLW)
Descriptors: *College Students; *Computers; Data Processing; Higher Education; *Time Management; Use Studies; *Word Processing; *Writing (Composition)
Identifiers: *Computer Centers; Yale University CT

Education Journal (EJ) identification number

EJ298427 IR512505 ——*Title*
A Dyslexic Can Compose on a Computer. ——*Author*
Arms, Valarie M.
Educational Technology, v24 n1 p39-41 Jan 1984 ——*Journal publication data*
Available from: UMI
Language: English
Document Type: PROJECT DESCRIPTION (141)
Journal Announcement: CIJAUG84

Abstract— Describes the strategies used by a technical writing teacher who encouraged a dyslexic university engineering student to use a microcomputer as an aid in composition writing, and discusses how a word processing program was used to make the writing process easier and increase the student's self-confidence. (MBR)

Subject headings Descriptors: College Students; Computer Assisted Instruction; *Dyslexia; Higher Education; Learning Disabilities; Learning Motivation; *Microcomputers; *Teaching Methods; *Word Processing; *Writing (Composition)

EJ298270 FL515801
Computer-Assisted Text-Analysis for ESL Students.
Reid, Joy; And Others
CALICO Journal, v1 n3 p40-42 Dec 1983
Language: English
Document Type: PROJECT DESCRIPTION (141); POSITION PAPER (120)
Journal Announcement: CIJAUG84
Reports an investigation into possibilities of using word processors and text analysis software with English as second language (ESL) students to determine (1) if foreign students can learn to use computer equipment, (2) if students feel time invested is worthwhile, and (3) if ESL students' problems with writing American academic prose can be remedied by this type of assistance. (SL)
Descriptors: Comparative Analysis; *Computer Assisted Instruction; *English (Second Language); Grammar; Modern Language Curriculum; Second Language Learning; *Student Participation; Vocabulary Development; *Word Processing; *Writing Skills

EJ298267 FL515798
Computer-Assisted Language Learning at the University of Dundee.
Lewis, Derek R.
CALICO Journal, v1 n3 p10-12 Dec 1983
Language: English
Document Type: NON-CLASSROOM MATERIAL (055); POSITION PAPER (120)
Journal Announcement: CIJAUG84
Presents an overview of activities in field of computer-assisted language learning at the University of Dundee (Scotland). These include: (1) use and testing of a self-instructional teacher's package, (2) development of the computer-controlled tape recorder, (3) cloze-type gapping exercises, and (4) projects aimed at the word processing translation skills of undergraduates. (SL)
Descriptors: *Cloze Procedure; *Computer Assisted Instruction; Foreign Countries; *Language Tests; Modern Language Curriculum; *Second Language Instruction; *Student Participation; Translation; Undergraduate Students; *Word Processing; Writing Skills
Identifiers: Dundee University (Scotland)

FIGURE 2-6 Online Database

particular database you are using. ERIC on-disk, for example, uses the "ERIC Descriptors" as its method of cataloging by subject.

ACCESSING INFORMATION FROM OTHER LIBRARIES

If, in your search, you discover that some item you need is not located in your library, it is still possible to find the item in another library. An online computer database called the OCLC (Online Computer Library Center) provides thousands of libraries with connections to each other's catalogs. By searching the OCLC database (by author or title), you can quickly ascertain if a nearby library contains the needed item; then you may request it through interlibrary loan or secure it yourself.

DISCIPLINE-SPECIFIC RESOURCES FOR SOCIAL SCIENCE

General Sources and Guides to Literature

The Annual Register: A Record of World Events. H. G. Hodson, ed. Detroit: Gale, 1980–present. For any given year, a record is kept of major events happening in the world.

A Bibliographical Guide to Education. New York Public Library staff editors. New York: G. K. Hall, 1985. A guide to sources for education topics.

Family Facts at Your Fingertips. C. A. Thacher. Salt Lake City, UT: Hawkes, 1987. Useful, up-to-date statistics about families.

Guide to Library Research in Psychology. J. E. Bell. Dubuque, IA: Wm. C. Brown, 1971. A useful source for undergraduate research in psychology.

Guide to Library Sources in Political Science: American Government. C. A. Vose. San Antonio, TX: American Political, 1975. A useful source for undergraduate research in American government and politics.

Information Sources in Education and Work. K. Dibden and J. Tomlinson, eds. Stoneham, MA: Butterworth, 1981.

Information Sources in Politics and Political Science: A Survey Worldwide. D. Englefield and G. Drewry, eds. Stoneham, MA: Butterworth, 1984.

Information Sources of Political Science. 4th ed. F. Holler. Santa Barbara, CA: ABC-Clio, 1986. Lists and annotates reference sources, including specific areas of political science.

The Literature of Political Science: A Guide for Students, Librarians, and Teachers. C. Brock. New York: Bowker, 1969.

The Student Anthropologist's Handbook. C. Frantz. Cambridge, MA: Schenkman, 1972. A guide to the discipline, including research materials.

The Student Sociologist's Handbook. 4th ed. P. Bart and L. Frankel. New York: Random House, 1986. Useful source for undergraduate research in sociology.

Study of International Relations: A Guide to Information Sources. R. Pfaltzgraff, Jr., ed. Detroit: Gale, 1977. A guide for students of international politics.

Dictionaries and Almanacs

Almanac of American History. A. M. Schlesinger, Jr., ed. New York: G. P. Putnam's, 1983. Provides facts and data on American history.

Almanac of American Politics, 1990. M. Barone, G. Ujifusa, ed. Washington, D.C.: National Journal. Provides facts and data on American politics for each year—updated annually.

Congressional Quarterly Almanac. Washington, D.C.: Congressional Quarterly, 1945–present. Summarizes the yearly activities of Congress, including voting records and major legislation.

Dictionary of American History, rev. ed. Martin et al., eds. New York: Rowman, 1990. Defines terms and discusses briefly subjects of interest in American history.

Dictionary of Anthropology. C. Winick. Totowa, NJ: Littlefield, 1977. Provides information on anthropological topics.

Dictionary of Behavioral Sciences, 2nd ed. B. Wolman, ed. New York: Van Nostrand Reinhold, 1989. Provides simple and concise definitions of terms in psychology and related fields.

Dictionary of Education. D. Rowntree. New York: B&N Imports, 1982. Concise definitions of terminology in education.

Dictionary of Political Thought. Roger Scrutin. New York: Hill & Wang, 1984.

Dictionary of Psychology, 2nd ed. J. Chaplin. New York: Viking, 1985. Provides concise definitions of psychological terms.

Handbooks

Handbook of Developmental Psychology. B. Wolman, ed. Englewood Cliffs, NJ: Prentice-Hall, 1982. Guide to issues and information in human development.

Handbook of Educational Technology: A Practical Guide for Teachers, 2nd ed. F. Percival and H. Ellington. New York: Nichols, 1988. Guide to terms in educational technology.

Historian's Handbook: A Key to the Study of Writing of History, 2nd ed. W. Gray et al. New York: Houghton Mifflin, 1991. Useful guide for undergraduates in history.

International Yearbook of Education. Lanham, MD: Bernan-Unipub, annual. 1979–present. Each year, a new topic in education is covered; for example, the 1984 yearbook theme was "Education for Life."

Political Handbook of the World. 1982–present (annual). A. S. Banker et al., eds. Binghamton, NY: CSA. Summaries of world political events.

United States Government Manual. Washington, D.C.: U.S. Government Printing Office, 1934–present. Provides current information on all aspects of the federal government.

Encyclopedia

Encyclopedia of Educational Research. M. Alkin, ed. New York: Macmillan, 1992. Excellent summaries of research in education.

Encyclopedia of Human Development and Education. R. Thomas, ed. New York: Pergamon, 1990. Contains terms, theories, and information on topics related to development and education.

Encyclopedia of Policy Studies. Nagel (Public Administration and Public Policy Services). New York: Dekker, 1983. Contains information about public policy issues.

Encyclopedia of Psychology. R. Corsini. New York: Wiley, 1984. Provides an overview of important terms and concepts in psychology.

Encyclopedia of Social Work. 18th ed. A. Minahan, ed. New York: National Association of Social Workers, 1965–present. Provides general information on a variety of topics related to social work. Includes both articles and biographies.

Encyclopedia of Sociology. Borgata and Borgata. New York: Macmillan, 1991. Describes terms, concepts, major ideas, major theorists in sociology.

International Encyclopedia of Education. Husen and Postlethwaite. New York: Pergamon, 1985. Provides background information on topics related to higher education (education beyond high school).

International Encyclopedia of Politics and Law. Published by Archives Publishers. New York: State Mutual Book and Periodicals Services, 1987.

International Encyclopedia of Psychiatry, Psychology, Psychoanalysis, and Neurology. 12 vols. B. B. Wolman, ed. New York: Van Nostrand Reinhold, 1977. Provides concise information on psychology and related fields.

International Encyclopedia of the Social Sciences. 8 vols. plus supplements. D. L. Sills, ed. New York: Macmillan, 1977. Provides analyses of current topics and issues in the social sciences. Includes a biographical supplement published in 1979.

Man, Myth, and Magic. R. Cavendish, ed. New York: Marshall Cavendish, 1983. An illustrated encyclopedia of mythology, religion, and the unknown.

Biographies

Biographical Dictionary of American Educators. 3 vols. J. F. Ohles, ed. Westport, CT: Greenwood, 1978.

Biographical Dictionary of Modern Peace Leaders. H. Jacobsen et al., eds. Westport, CT: Greenwood, 1985. Provides concise biographies about important figures in the peace movement around the world.

Biographical Dictionary of Psychology. L. Zasne. Westport, CT: Greenwood, 1984. Provides concise biographies about important psychologists.

Statesman's Yearbook. New York: St. Martin's, 1975–present. Provides concise information about important political leaders in any given year.

Who's Who in American Politics. 10th ed. Compiled by J. Cattell. New York: Bowker, 1985 plus annual updates. Discusses important figures in American politics each year.

Indexes and Abstracts

ANTHROPOLOGY

Abstracts in Anthropology

ASIAN STUDIES

Bibliography of Asian Studies
*Public Affairs Information Services Bulletin (PAIS)

BLACK STUDIES

Black Index: Afro-Americans in Selected Periodicals
Index to Periodical Articles by and about Negroes

* = Computer searching available

CRIME

Abstracts on Criminology and
    Penology
Criminology and Penology Abstracts

EDUCATION

Child Development Abstracts and
    Bibliography
*Current Index to Journals in
    Education
Deaf, Speech, Hearing Abstracts
Educational Administration Abstracts
*Education Index
*ERIC on Disc
*Exceptional Child Education
    Resources
Physical Education Index
Physical Fitness/Sports Medicine
*Resources in Education
*Resources in Vocational Education
State Education Journal Index

FAMILY STUDIES

Inventory of Marriage and Family
    Literature
Sage Family Studies Abstracts

LAW

Current Law Index
Index to Legal Periodicals

LIBRARY SCIENCE

*Library and Information Science
    Abstracts
*Library Literature
Library Science Abstracts
Library Technology Report

POLITICAL SCIENCE

ABC Political Science
Combined Retrospective Index to
    Journals in Political Science
Congressional Quarterly Weekly
    Reports
International Political Science
    Abstracts
*Public Affairs Information Service
    Bulletin

PSYCHOLOGY

*Psychological Abstracts

SOCIAL SCIENCES—GENERAL

Consumer's Index
*Public Affairs Information Service
*Social Science Citation Index
*Social Science Index

SOCIOLOGY AND SOCIAL WORK

Combined Retrospective Index to
    Journals in Sociology
Index to Current Urban Documents
Rehabilitation Literature
Social Work Research and Abstracts
*Sociological Abstracts
Women's Studies Abstracts
*World Agricultural Economics and
    Rural Sociology Abstracts

TRANSPORTATION

Highway Research Abstracts
Highway Safety Literature
Transportation Research Abstracts

UNITED NATIONS

Specialized Agency Catalogs
United Nations Documents Index

**U.S. CONGRESS AND U.S.
GOVERNMENT**

*American Statistics Index (ASI)
CIS Annual Index to Congressional
    Publications of Legislative
    Histories
CIS U.S. Congressional Committee
    Prints Index
Commerce Clearing House Congres-
    sional Index
*Congressional Information Service
Congressional Quarterly Almanac
Index to U.S. Government Periodicals
*Monthly Catalog of U.S. Govern-
    ment Publications
*U.S. Government Reports, An-
    nouncements and Index (NTIS)

◆ **EXERCISES**

1. Using the *Social Sciences Index*, or another index appropriate for your field, look up a current issue, for example, a social problem (alcoholism, child abuse, or prison reform). Find the title of one current article in a scholarly journal. Write down or print out the citation from the index, find the complete journal name in the front of the index, and using that information find the journal article in your library. (Remember, you will need to look up the journal name in the serials listing just as you did for a popular magazine.) Make a photocopy of the article. On your copy, underline key ideas. Then construct an outline of the article. Turn in the photocopy with your outline.

2. Find any information your library has about online computer searches and discuss computer searching in your particular field with the librarian responsible for computer searches.

3. Find out whether your library has any databases on videodisk or CD-ROM that you can search using a microcomputer. Try out any such tools, using appropriate subject headings and key words for your topic, and turn in the printout generated from your search.

4. Interview one of your professors about library research in his or her field. How does that professor gather information needed for his or her work? How has the research process changed over the years? How much does the professor rely on computer searching? Write a short paragraph summarizing the interview.

5. Interview a reference librarian at your campus library. How has information access changed? How many new information sources have come to campus in the past year or so? What does the librarian foresee in the libraries of the future? Write a short paragraph summarizing the interview.

3

◆ ◆ ◆

Library Research Methods

Successful research depends on knowing what library resources are available, but it also depends on knowing how to find and use those resources. Developing a search strategy will help you to find materials on your research topic and to use library resources efficiently. First, you need to use library tools to locate source materials; then you must evaluate those sources and interpret them so that they will be useful to your particular research project.

PREPARATION AND INCUBATION

As a college student, you are uniquely prepared to conduct a research project. Your experiences and prior schooling have given you a wealth of information to draw from. A research project may begin in one of the following ways: you may have been assigned to do a research paper in a particular college class or you may have discovered an interesting question or problem on your own that you decided to investigate. Although the former impetus, a course assignment, might seem artificial or contrived at first, in reality it may give you the opportunity to investigate something that has always intrigued you.

Finding a Topic

A good place to begin looking for a research topic is in the textbooks you are currently using for the courses you are taking. Scan the table of contents with an eye toward a topic that you'd enjoy investigating. Or if you have no idea at all, begin by browsing through a specialized encyclopedia, such as the *Encyclopedia of Psychology* or the *Encyclopedia of Education.* A third resource for finding topics is Editorial Research Reports (ERR). If your library subscribes to ERR, it receives a weekly description of a wide variety of contemporary events, problems, and issues, such as acid rain, homelessness, or women in business. A bibliography listing several recent articles, books, and reports on each topic covered by ERR is also included. Skimming these reports may spark an interest in a particular topic, as well as get you started on finding relevant materials and information.

Once you have an idea for a topic, you might discuss your idea with a reference librarian, with your teacher, and with other students in your class. They may have ideas or suggestions related to your topic or may be able to direct you to aspects of the topic you may not have considered. Your goal is to focus your topic by asking pertinent starting questions that your research will attempt to answer. So, if your general topic is "acid rain," your specific starting question might be "What have the effects of acid rain been on the forests of New York?" Or, "What is the EPA currently doing to control pollutants that cause acid rain?" Such questions, which should be neither too trivial nor too broad, will help you to sort through information in search of an answer and may prevent you from aimlessly reading on a topic area that is too general.

Gathering Research Materials

The Research Notebook

To keep track of all your research, you need to obtain a notebook to serve as your "research notebook." In the notebook, you record your specific topic area and the starting questions you wish to answer, outline your plans for searching the library (called a library search strategy), and begin a list of sources (called a working bibliography). Your research notebook is also the place where you can begin to articulate for yourself your own understanding of the answer to your starting question as it evolves through your research. It is crucial that, as you investigate your topic, you record in the research notebook not only what others have said on the subject, but also your own impressions and comments.

Your research notebook, then, will be the place for tracing your entire research process: the starting questions, the search strategy, the sources used in your search, your notes, reactions to and comments on the sources, the tentative answers you propose to your starting question, a thesis statement articulating the main points to be covered by your paper, an informal outline or an organizational plan for your paper, and all preliminary drafts of your paper. Many students like to take notes from sources in their research notebooks instead of on note-cards, in order to keep all their research information in a single convenient place. If you decide on this approach, be sure to record your notes and evaluative comments in separate parts of the notebook. I suggest to my students that they leave a blank page for comments in their notebooks adjacent to each page of notes. Also, remember to reserve a place in your notebook for recording any primary research data (such as interview, survey, or questionnaire data) that you collect in connection with your research project.

A Computer Research Notebook

If you are using a word processor, you can take advantage of the storage capabilities of your computer to develop a computer research notebook. Create a file or directory on your computer and label it your research notebook file. All of the items previously listed for a research notebook can be gathered together in this one file or directory on your computer. For example, you could include your topic and starting questions, search strategy, working bibliography, notes and evaluative comments on sources, and so on. In this way, your research project can proceed systematically as you gather information and build your own expertise on your topic through your evolving computer file. Using word processing, then, you can revise your notebook file, organize your information, and even write your paper based on the stored information on disk.

For example, a student who had to write a research report for a computer science class decided to write about computer crime. In thinking about the subject, he determined that first he needed to categorize the types of computer crimes so that he could arrange the information in his research notebook in an organized way. As he read books and articles on the subject, he began to sort materials into the following subheadings: computer as object or target of crime, computer as subject or site of crime, computer as instrument used to create crime, and computer as symbol for criminal deception or intimidation. After entering these subheadings onto his computer file, he gradually built up the report; as he encountered information for the various sections of his report, he added it under the appropriate subheading in his file. You could use a similar method for your own research notebook.

The Working Bibliography

A bibliography, as you learned in Chapter 2, is a list of books and articles on a particular subject. Your working bibliography, your preliminary list of sources, grows as your research progresses, as one source leads you to another. It is called a "working" bibliography—as opposed to the finished bibliography—because it may contain some sources that you ultimately will not use in your paper.

A working bibliography need not be in final bibliographic form, but it is important to record accurately all the information eventually needed to compose your final bibliography to keep from having to backtrack and find a book or article again. Oftentimes, a student finds a book, reads a relevant section and takes notes, but neglects to write down all of the bibliographic information, that is, the author(s), complete title, publisher, date and place of publication, and so on (see pp. 20–21). Then, when compiling the final bibliography in which are listed all of the sources referred to in the paper, the student discovers that he or she has not written down the date of publication, for instance, or the author's first name. This means another trip to the library to find the book or journal, which may or may not still be on the shelf!

The working bibliography should be comprehensive, the place where you note down all sources that you run across—in bibliographies or databases, for example, whether your library has them and whether they turn out to be relevant to your topic. So, the working bibliography is a complete record of every possible path you encountered in your search, whether or not you ultimately followed that path. In contrast, the final bibliography lists only those sources that you actually read and used as references for your own paper.

The example below of a working bibliography comes from a student's research project on childhood schizophrenia.

Working Bibliography

Allen, J. (1985). Development of schizophrenia.
  Menninger Perspective, 2, 8–11.

Davidoff, L. (1984). Childhood psychosis. In the
  Encyclopedia of psychology (Vol. 10,
  pp. 156–157). New York: J. Wiley & Sons.

Goldfarb, W. (1961). Childhood schizophrenia.
  Cambridge, MA: Harvard University Press.

Kulick, E. (1985). Treatment of schizophrenia.
  Menninger Perspective, 2, 12–14.

MacDonald, A. (1982, Winter). Schizophrenia: The
  solitary nightmare. Highwire Magazine,
  pp. 37–38.

Stephens, R. (1984, March). Adam: A child's courageous battle against mental illness. <u>Family Circle</u>, pp. 98–102.

Torrey, F. (1983). <u>Surviving schizophrenia</u>. New York: Harper & Row.

Developing a Search Strategy

Once you have decided on some starting questions and have gathered the necessary research materials, you are ready to outline a preliminary search strategy. Many library research projects begin in the reference area of the library, since the library tools that refer you to other sources are kept there. Often you will begin with reference works (dictionaries, encyclopedias, and biographies), in which can be found background and contextualizing information on your topic. Then, you may proceed to more specific reference works (abstracts, indexes, and databases). To make your library search an orderly and thorough process, you should design a search strategy, beginning with general sources and working to more specific sources. In most fields, a search strategy includes the following major components:

1. Background sources—dictionaries and encyclopedias (including discipline-specific sources)
2. Biographies (on people relevant to your topic)
3. Reviews of literature and research reports (to discover how others outline or overview the subject)
4. Print indexes and bibliographies (for listings of source materials by subject) (Remember to use the LCSH for subject headings)
5. Library online catalog and other databases (including CD-ROMs) for subject and keyword searching of books and journal articles on your topic (Use your library's serials listing to locate sources available in your library)
6. Primary research (for firsthand information such as interviews or surveys)

The student researching childhood schizophrenia designed the following search strategy to help her begin her research:

Kristen's Search Strategy

1. Encyclopedias, dictionaries, and textbooks for general background information including the *Encyclopedia of Psychology* and the *Encyclopedic Dictionary of Psychology*.

2. Library's computerized online catalog for a subject search on childhood schizophrenia, using headings from the LCSH.
3. A database search of WSOC, the social science database, in addition to print subject indexes for access to magazine and journal articles on childhood schizophrenia.
4. Abstracts of scholarly sources from *Psychological Abstracts* using PsychLit on CD-ROM.

Notice that this student's search began in the reference area and ended with use of the online catalog. Many students make the mistake of using the catalog before they really know enough about their topics to make it useful. You would be wise to order your search strategy to begin in the reference area as well.

You may need to change or modify your search strategy as you go along; do not feel that the strategy must be rigid or inflexible. However, using a search strategy enables you to proceed in an orderly, systematic fashion with your research. On your working bibliography, write down the complete citation for each source you encounter in your search. As you read in the general and specialized encyclopedias, for example, you may find related references listed at the end of articles. Write down in your working bibliography complete citations for any references that look promising so that you can look them up later. Similarly, as you look through the reviews, the indexes, and the card catalog, write down the citations to any promising sources. In this way, you will build your working bibliography during your library search.

✦ EXERCISES

To begin preparation for your own research project, follow these steps:

1. Select and narrow a research topic, that is, limit the topic in scope so that it is of a manageable size. Talk your topic over with others, including your classmates, your teacher, and your librarians.
2. Articulate several starting questions that you would seek to answer during your research.
3. Gather your research materials—notebook and notecards. Or create a computer file or directory for a computerized notebook.
4. Reserve space in your research notebook or computer file for both notes from sources and the evaluative comments that you will write down as you are reading.

5. Reserve space in your research notebook or computer file for your working bibliography in which you will list all of the sources you encounter during your search.
6. Outline your search strategy (refer to Chapter 2 for specific library resources).

Outlining a Time Frame

After writing down your search strategy, you will have at least some idea of how long your research is likely to take. Now is the time to sit down with a calendar and create a time frame for your entire research project. Your teacher may have given you some deadlines, and if so, they will help you decide on a time frame. If not, you will have to set your own dates for accomplishing specific tasks so that you can proceed in an orderly fashion toward the completion of the project. If you have never done a research project before, you might be overwhelmed at the thought of such a large task. However, if you break the job down into smaller parts, it will seem more manageable.

Allow yourself three to four weeks for locating, reading, and evaluating sources. As you begin to work in the library, you will see that a library search is a very time-consuming process. Just locating sources in a large library takes time; perhaps one book you need will be shelved in the third sub-basement and another on the fourth floor! Sometimes a book you want will have been checked out; in such a case you will have to submit a "recall notice" to the librarian asking that the book be returned and reserved for you. You may also find that you need to obtain materials from another library through an interlibrary loan, another time-consuming process. Plan to spend two to three hours in the library each day for the first month of your research project. After that, you may find you can spend less time in the library.

If your research project involves primary research (see Chapter 4), begin to plan for that research while you are writing your search strategy. Allow one to two weeks for conducting your primary research, depending on its nature and scope.

Schedule one to two weeks for preliminary writing. To make sense of your subject and answer your starting question, you need to spend time and effort in studying and evaluating your sources, in brainstorming and writing discovery drafts. Eventually, you ought to be able to express your understanding of the subject in a thesis statement, which helps control the shape and direction of the research paper and provides your readers with a handle on your paper's main idea or argument.

Finally, give yourself enough time to plan, organize, and write the complete draft of your research paper. You need time to plan or outline your paper and to construct your argument, using your source information to reinforce or substantiate your findings in a clearly documented way. Allow yourself one to two weeks for organizing and writing rough drafts of your paper and an additional week for revising, polishing, and editing your final draft. If you intend to hire a typist or if you need to type your paper in what may turn out to be a busy computer lab, allow an extra week for the typing of the paper.

As you can see from this overview, most research projects take an entire college term to complete. Recall from Chapter 1 the stages in the research process: preparation, incubation, illumination, and verification. You need to consider all four stages as you plan your research project. Allow time for your library search, time for ideas to incubate in your subconscious, time for arriving at an understanding of your topic, and time to verify that understanding in writing.

What follows is a sample time frame to give you some idea of how you might budget your own time:

Week 1:   Select preliminary research topic; articulate starting questions; gather and organize research notebook; draw up tentative search strategy; plan research time frame; read general background sources; begin to focus topic.

Week 2:   Build working bibliography by using indexes, online catalogs, and databases; begin to locate sources in library.

Week 3:   Read and evaluate sources; take notes on relevant sources; in research notebook, comment on sources, that is, their importance to topic and their relationship to other sources.

Week 4:   Arrange and conduct any primary research; complete reading and evaluating of sources; identify gaps in research and find more sources if necessary.

Week 5:   Begin preliminary writing in research notebook—summary, synthesis, critique activities; initiate brainstorming and discovery drafting; begin to define an answer to the starting question.

Week 6:   Write a tentative thesis statement; sketch a tentative plan or outline of the research paper.

Week 7:   Write a rough draft of the research paper; keep careful track of sources through accurate citation (distinguish quotes from paraphrases).

Week 8:   Revise and edit the rough draft; spellcheck; check correct usage and documentation of sources.

Week 9:   Print and proofread final copy carefully; have a friend or classmate proof as well.

✦ EXERCISES

1. Outline the time frame of your research project; refer to a current academic calendar from your school and to any deadlines provided by your teacher.

2. Plan any primary research you intend to conduct for your project. For example, if you need to contact someone for an interview, do so well ahead of time.

WORKING WITH SOURCES

One of the most crucial aspects of the research process is the development of the skills needed to pull the appropriate information from the source materials you have gathered.

Reading for Meaning

The sources you locate in your library search are the raw material for your research paper. You might supplement these sources with primary data, but generally your research paper will be based on information from written secondary sources. Your job is to read carefully and actively. Reading is not a passive process by which the words float into your mind and become registered in your memory. If you read passively, you will not comprehend the author's message. You have probably had the experience of rereading a passage several times and still not understanding a word of it. In such cases, you were not reading actively. In active reading, the reader is engaged in a dialogue with the author.

To be fair in your interpretation of what you are reading, you must first be receptive to what the author is saying; approach anything you read with an open mind. Before actually beginning to read, look at any nontextual materials that accompany the source, including information about the author, the publisher, the origin of the work, the title, and the organizational plan or format of the work.

The Author.   Questions to consider about the author include the following: Who is the author? Is the author living or dead? What other works did the author write? What are the author's qualifications and biases on this particular topic? Is the author affiliated with any organizations that might espouse a particular point of view (e.g., the National Rifle Association or the National Organization for Women)? Is the author a faculty member at a reputable college or university? Does the author work for a government agency, a political group, or an industry?

The Publication.   You should look at the publication information for the source. What was the date of publication? Would the particular context help you understand the work? It is also important to evaluate the medium in which the work appears. Was this an article published in a popular magazine, such as *Ladies' Home Journal*, or was it a paper in a scholarly journal, such as *College and Research Libraries*? The title of the work itself may reveal some important information. Does the title seem significant? Does it indicate the probable conclusions or main points of the article or book? Does it provide a clue to some controversy? Authors provide titles as indicators of what the work will contain, so we should be sensitive to the title of any work we read.

The Organization.   Finally, before you read the work, look at the author's organizational plan. For a book, look at the table of contents, the introduction or preface, the chapter headings, and the major subdivisions. Judging from these clues, ask yourself what the author's main points are likely to be. What does the author seem to consider important about the subject? For articles, read the abstract (if provided) and look at any subdivisions or headings. These will help you to understand the overall structure of the article.

Active Reading and Notetaking

Once you have completed your preliminary overview of the work, you are ready to begin the actual reading process. Plan to read a work that you need to understand thoroughly at least twice. During the first reading, go through the work at a relatively quick pace, either a section or a chapter at a time. If an article is relatively short, you can read it through entirely at one sitting. As you go along, pay attention to key words or phrases and try to get a general idea of the author's main points. This reading will be more than a skimming of the work; you should be able to generally understand what you have read on this first time through.

Then read the work again, carefully and slowly. Use a highlighter or a pencil to underline key ideas and to write in the margins of your own books or photocopied articles, called annotating the article. Of course, if you are borrowing a book from the library, you will not be able to underline on the book itself. In that case, record key ideas, using your own words, on your notecards or in your research notebook, along with the author's name and the page number on which the material was found. The second time you read, stop frequently to absorb the information and interpret it in your own mind. For each paragraph or section of the article or chapter, jot down on the page itself or on notecards a summary sentence or two that captures the main idea. Be sure that these marginal notes are in your own words. It is crucial that you paraphrase the author's ideas and that you note down the page number on which you found the information.

Paraphrasing Appropriately and Avoiding Plagiarism

Paraphrasing. Paraphrasing may be defined as restating or rewording a passage from a text, giving the same meaning in another form. The objective of paraphrasing, then, is to present an author's ideas in your own words. When paraphrasing fails, it may be because the reader misunderstood the passage, the reader insisted on reading his or her own ideas into the passage, or the reader partially understood but chose to guess at the meaning rather than fully understanding it. To paraphrase accurately, you must first read closely and understand completely what you are reading. Here are five suggestions that will help you as you paraphrase:

1. Place the information found in the source in a new order.
2. Break the complex ideas into smaller units of meaning.
3. Use concrete, direct vocabulary in place of technical jargon found in the original source.
4. Vary the sentence patterns.
5. Use synonyms for the words in the source.

Plagiarism. Plagiarism is defined as the unauthorized use of the language and thoughts of an author and the representation of them as one's own. Oftentimes students taking notes from a source will inadvertently commit plagiarism by careless copying of words and phrases from the author that end up in the student's paper and appear as if written by the student himself or herself. If you set the original piece aside while you are taking notes, you are less likely to copy the author's wording. Then go back and double check your notes against the original.

Sometimes plagiarism is not inadvertent at all, but rather overt theft of one author's work by another, as the accompanying article by Gregg Easterbrook attests. However, whether the plagiarist is a Stanford author or a newspaper reporter, it is always unethical to present someone's words or ideas as if they were your own. Nor is providing a footnote alone always sufficient. Any of the author's words or phrases should be enclosed in quotation marks to signal to the reader that exact wording and phrasing as written by the original author is being used; in addition, a footnote or parenthetical citation to the source should be provided.

The Sincerest Flattery

Thanks, but I'd rather you not plagiarize my work

Gregg Easterbrook

It was the best of times, and pretty much the worst of times. I felt borne back ceaselessly to the past. Maybe that's because days on the calendar creep along in a petty pace, and all our yesterdays but light fools the road to dusty death.

OK, the above words are not really mine. But hey, I changed them slightly. I thought nobody would notice.

Some kind of harmonic convergence of plagiarism seems to be in process. A Boston University dean, H. Joachim Maitre, was caught swiping much of a commencement address from an essay by the film critic Michael Medved. Fox Butterfield of *The New York Times* then cribbed from a *Boston Globe* story about the swipe. *The Globe,* in turn, admitted that one of its reporters was disciplined for stealing words from the Georgia politician Julian Bond. Laura Parker of *The Washington Post* (which owns NEWSWEEK) was found poaching from *The Miami Herald*'s John Donnelly. And the president of Japan's largest news service, Shinji Sakai, announced his resignation, taking public responsibility for 51 plagiarized articles that were discovered last May.

I personally entered the arena last week when the *Post* reported that a Stanford University business-school lecturer plagiarized me in a recent book, "Managing on the Edge." Chapters about the Ford Motor Co. contain approximately three pages nearly identical in wording to an article on Ford that I wrote five years ago for *The Washington Monthly* magazine.

What's it like to discover someone has stolen your words? My initial reaction was to feel strangely flattered that another author had liked my writing well enough to pass it off as his own.

OK, I plagiarized that last sentence. It comes from the writer James Fallows, who last week in a National Public Radio commentary described the two times he has been plagiarized. In one case a San Jose State professor published a textbook in which an entire chapter was nearly identical to an article Fallows had written. For good measure, another chapter was nearly identical to an article by the economic analyst Robert Reich. The professor claims this happened because of computer error. The publisher sent Fallows a letter saying that, since we disseminated your copyrighted work without permission, could we have permission now?

Plagiarism is the world's dumbest crime. If you are caught there is absolutely nothing you can say in your own defense. (Computer error?) And it's easy to commit the underlying sin—presenting as your own someone else's work—without running the risk of sanction, merely by making the effort to reword.

Yet figures as distinguished as Alex Haley, John Hersey, Martin Luther King Jr., and D. M. Thomas have been charged with borrowing excessively from the work of others. One factor is sloth. Another is ego: there are writers who cannot bear even tacit admission that someone else has said something better than they could. The line between being influenced by what others have written, and cribbing from it outright, is one nearly every writer walks up to at some point.

About that last sentence. *The Post* quoted me as saying that: does that mean I just plagiarized myself? It can happen. Conor Cruise O'Brien was accused of self-plagiarizing when he sold, to The Atlantic, an article hauntingly similar to one previously run under his byline in Harper's.

Perhaps word rustlers tell themselves they will never be caught, and indeed, unlikely combinations of events may be necessary for a theft to be exposed. Some no doubt further tell themselves that if they are caught no one will sue. Most writers don't make serious money and so are uninviting targets for litigation.

I might never have learned about "Managing on the Edge" if an alert reader named Robert Levering had not been researching Ford Motor Co. Shortly after reading my article, he saw a "Managing" excerpt from the Stanford business-school magazine. He not only realized he was reading the same words, but more important, remembered where he encountered them first. Levering wrote to Stanford. I heard about his letter, got a copy of the book, and my jaw dropped. Particularly galling, on the book's facing page, was the phrase "Copyright 1990 by Richard Tanner Pascale." The author was asserting ownerships of words I composed.

Elegantly crafted: Unlike the Boston University incident, where the dean stole words for an unpaid speech, in this case there was money involved. "Managing" is a commercial book published by Simon & Schuster, a reasonable seller with 35,000 copies in print and another run pending. It's been well received by critics: mainly, I suspect, because of three particularly elegantly crafted pages. Another person was not only presenting my words as his own, but doing so for gain.

The author of "Managing" apologized for what happened but contended it was not plagiarism, because my name is in the book's footnotes. Footnotes my foot. Footnotes mean the place a fact can be found; they do not confer the right to present someone else's words as your own work. Any Stanford undergraduate who attempted that defense would not get far.

My case dragged on inconclusively for a while. But the moment a reporter for *The Washington Post* called Simon & Schuster, the pace of cooperation accelerated dramatically. Simon & Schuster is now preparing corrections for future editions of "Managing." Stanford has an academic committee investigating its end of the incident.

The wave of plagiarism disclosures poses an obvious question: are dozens of authors now quaking in their shoes, worried about whether some alert reader will stumble across the resemblance between those pages in their book and, say, that article in some obscure little journal no one ever reads?

Frankly, Scarlet, I don't give a damn. ✦

Easterbrook, G. (1991, July 29). The sincerest flattery: Thanks, but I'd rather you not plagiarize my work. *Newsweek*, pp. 45-46.

How to Paraphrase Appropriately

The examples below show acceptable and unacceptable paraphrasing:

ORIGINAL PASSAGE

During the last two years of my medical course and the period which I spent in the hospitals as house physician, I found time, by means of serious encroachment on my night's rest, to bring to completion a work on the history of scientific research into the thought world of St. Paul, to revise and enlarge the *Question of the Historical Jesus* for the second edition, and together with Widor to prepare an edition of Bach's preludes and fugues for the organ, giving with each piece directions for its rendering. (Albert Schweitzer, *Out of My Life and Thought*. New York: Mentor, 1963, p. 94.)

A POOR PARAPHRASE

    Schweitzer said that during the last two
years of his medical course and the period he
spent in the hospitals as house physician he
found time, by encroaching on his night's rest,
to bring to completion several works.

[Note: This paraphrase uses too many words and phrases directly from the original without putting them in quotation marks and thus is considered plagiarism. Furthermore, many of the ideas of

Embarrassing Echoes

I n both journalism and academia, plagiarism is close to mortal sin.
Sometimes writers are tempted to stray, giving themselves credit for
the work of another. A side-by-side comparison can be withering.

Gregg Easterbrook, Oct. 1986:	**Richard Pascale, March, 1990**
"On a very dark day in 1980, Donald Peterson, newly chosen president of Ford Motors, visited the company design studios. Ford was in the process of losing $2.2 billion, the largest single-year corporate loss in U.S. history."	"On a dark day in 1980, Donald Peterson, the newly chosen President of Ford Motor Company, visited the company's Detroit design studio. That year, Ford would lose $2.2 billion, the largest loss in a single year in U.S. corporate history."

Sources: The Washington Monthly: "Managing on the Edge"

Michael Medved, Feb. 2, 1991:	**H. Joachim Maitre, May 12, 1991:**
"Apparently, some stern decree has gone out from the upper reaches of the Hollywood establishment that love between married people must never be portrayed on the screen."	"Apparently, some stern advice has come from the upper reaches of the Hollywood establishment that love between married people must never be portrayed on the screen."

Source: The Boston Globe

the author have been left out, making the paraphrase incomplete.
Finally, the student has neglected to acknowledge the source
through a parenthetical citation.]

A GOOD PARAPHRASE

        Albert Schweitzer observed that by staying

up late at night, first as a medical student and

then as a "house physician," he was able to

finish several major works, including a

historical book on the intellectual world of St.

Paul, a revised and expanded second edition of

Question of the Historical Jesus, and a new

edition of Bach's organ preludes and fugues

complete with interpretive notes, written

collaboratively with Widor (Schweitzer 94).

[Note: This paraphrase is very complete and appropriate; it does not use the author's own words, except in one instance, which is acknowledged by quotation marks. The student has included a parenthetical citation that indicates to the reader the paraphrase was taken from page 94 of the work by Schweitzer. The reader can find complete information on the work by turning to the bibliography at the end of the student's paper.]

Making Section-by-Section Summaries

As an alternative to close paraphrasing, you may wish to write brief summaries (three or four sentences) on your notecards or in your notebook. Again, use your own words when writing these summaries. If the material is particularly difficult, you may need to stop and summarize more frequently than after each section or chapter. If it is relatively simple to understand or not particularly pertinent to your topic, take fewer notes and write shorter summaries. At any rate, be certain that you are internalizing what you read—the best gauge of your understanding of the material is your ability to put it into your own words in the form of paraphrases or short section-by-section summaries. Again, as with paraphrases or quotes, note down the page numbers on which the material was found.

Reviewing

After completing your marginal notes, paraphrases, or summaries, go back and review the entire piece, taking time to think about what you read. Evaluate the significance of what you learned by relating the work to your own project and starting questions. Your research notebook is the place to record the observations and insights gained in your reading. How does the work fit in with other works you read on the same topic? What ideas seem particularly relevant to your own research? Does the work help to answer your starting question? Answering such questions in your research notebook will help you to put each work you read into the context of your own research.

Perceiving the Author's Organizational Plan

In writing, you should attempt to make your organizational plan clear to your potential readers. Similarly, while reading, you should attempt to discern the organizational plan of the author. One of the best ways to understand the author's plan is to try to reconstruct it through outlining. For an article or book that seems especially important to your research project, you may want to understand the material in a more complete and orderly way than that gained through paraphrasing or summarizing. You can accomplish this goal by constructing an outline of what you have read.

In a well-written piece, the writer will have given you clues to important or key information. Your summaries should have identified main ideas that are most likely to be the main points of the outline. However, you may still need to go back to the work to identify the author's secondary, supporting points, including examples, illustrations, and supporting arguments used to make each individual argument clearer or more persuasive. In outlining a key source, you can come to understand it more fully. Again, be sure that all the points in your outline have been stated in your own words rather than the words of the author.

✦ EXERCISE

The following article has been included to illustrate how to go about underlining, annotating, summarizing, and outlining a key source. Read the article carefully, noticing which ideas have been underlined and which annotated. Do you agree with my identification of key ideas? Why or why not? Is there a right or wrong identification of key ideas? The final third of the article has not been underlined, summarized, or included on the outline that follows. Try out these four techniques (underlining, annotating, summarizing, outlining) by finishing the interpretation of the article, beginning immediately after the quotation from Paul Dirac:

1. Underline key ideas.
2. Annotate the article by putting notes in the margins that paraphrase the author's words.
3. Summarize in your own words the main ideas of the last section of the article, as you would on a notecard or in your research notebook (three to four sentences).
4. Complete the outline following the article, using your own marginal notes and annotations on the article.

The Scientific Aesthetic

K. C. Cole

Opening quote from physics textbook.

"Poets say science takes away from the beauty of the stars—mere globs of gas atoms. Nothing is 'mere.' I too can see the stars on a desert night, and feel them. But do I see less or more? The vastness of the heavens stretches my imagination—stuck on this carrousel, my little eye can catch one-million-year-old light . . . For far more marvelous is the truth than any artists of the past imagined! Why do the poets of the present not speak of it? What men are poets who can speak of Jupiter if he were like a man, but if he is an immense spinning sphere of methane and ammonia must be silent?"

Feynman rejects idea that science makes nature ugly.

This poetic paragraph appears as a footnote in, of all places, a physics textbook: *The Feynman Lectures on Physics* by Nobel laureate Richard Feynman. Like so many others of his kind, <u>Feynman scorns the suggestion that science strips nature of her beauty,</u> leaving only a naked set of equations. Knowledge of nature, he thinks, deepens the awe, enhances the appreciation. But Feynman has also been known to remark that the only quality art and theoretical physics have in common is the <u>joyful anticipation that artists and physicists alike feel when they contemplate a blank piece of paper.</u>

There is both beauty and creativity in science and art, says Feynman.

What is the kinship between these seemingly dissimilar species, science and art? Obviously there is some—if only because so often the same people are attracted to both. The image of Einstein playing his violin is only too familiar, or Leonardo with his inventions. It is a standing joke in some circles that all it takes to make a string quartet is four mathematicians sitting in the same room. Even Feynman plays the bongo drums. (He finds it curious that while he is almost always identified as the physicist who plays the bongo drums, the few times that he has been asked to play the drums, "the introducer never seems to find it necessary to mention that I also do theoretical physics.")

What is the relationship between science and art? There must be a link, as so many scientists are also artists.

<u>One commonality is that art and science often cover the same territory. A tree is fertile ground for both the poet and the botanist.</u> The relationship between mother and child, the symmetry of snowflakes, the effects of light and color, and the structure of the human form are studied equally by painters and psychologists, sculptors and physicians. The origins of the universe, the nature of life, and the meaning of death are the subjects of physicists, philosophers, and composers.

Art and science cover same ground— examples.

Differing approaches: art = emotion, science = logic; but many scientists disagree, arguing that emotion in science is integral to the process.

Yet when it comes to approach, the affinity breaks down completely. Artists approach nature with feeling; scientists rely on logic. Art elicits emotion; science makes sense. Artists are supposed to care; scientists are supposed to think.

At least one physicist l know rejects this distinction out of hand: "What a strange misconception has been taught to people," he says. "They have been taught that one cannot be disciplined enough to discover the truth unless one is indifferent to it. Actually, there is no point in looking for the truth unless what it is makes a difference."

The history of science bears him out. Darwin, while sorting out the clues he had gathered in the Galapagos Islands that eventually led to his theory of evolution, was hardly detached. "I am like a gambler and love a wild experiment," he wrote. "I am horribly afraid." "I trust to a sort of instinct and God knows can seldom give any reason for my remarks." "All nature is perverse and will not do as I wish it. I wish I had my old barnacles to work at, and nothing new."

Examples of scientific passion— Einstein.

The scientists who took various sides in the early days of the quantum debate were scarcely less passionate. Einstein said that if classical notions of cause and effect had to be renounced, he would rather be a cobbler or even work in a gambling casino than be a physicist. Niels Bohr called Einstein's attitude appalling, and accused him of high treason. Another major physicist, Erwin Schrodinger, said, "If one has to stick to this damned quantum jumping, then I regret having ever been involved in this thing." On a more positive note, Einstein spoke about the universe as a "great, eternal riddle" that "beckoned like a liberation." As the late Harvard professor George Sarton wrote in the preface to his *History of Science*, "There are blood and tears in geometry as well as in art."

Artists and scientists are both passionate and in control of their work.

Instinctively, however, most people do not like the idea that scientists can be passionate about their work, any more than they like the idea that poets can be calculating. But it would be a sloppy artist indeed who worked without tight creative control, and no scientist ever got very far by sticking exclusively to the scientific method. Deduction only takes you to the next step in a straight line of thought, which in science is often a dead end. "Each time we get into this log jam," says Feynman, "it is because the methods we are using are just like the ones we have used before . . . A new idea is extremely difficult to think of. It takes fantastic imagination."

Creativity needed in science; control needed in art.

Scientists often proceed based on their own "vision of beauty."

Illustrations from science: aesthetics serve as "delicate sieve" for science.

<u>The direction of the next great leap is as often as not guided by the scientist's vision of beauty</u>. Einstein's highest praise for a theory was not that it was good but that it was beautiful. His strongest criticism was "Oh, how ugly!" He often spoke about the aesthetic appeal of ideas. "Pure logic could never lead us to anything but tautologies," wrote the French physicist Jules Henri Poincaré. "It could create nothing new; not from it alone can any science issue."

Poincaré also described the role that aesthetics plays in science as "a delicate sieve," an arbiter between the telling and the misleading, the signals and the distractions. Science is not a book of lists. The facts need to be woven into theories like tapestries out of so many tenuous threads. Who knows when (and how) the right connections have been made? <u>Sometimes, the most useful standard is aesthetic</u>: Erwin Schrodinger refrained from publishing the first version of his now famous wave equations because they did not fit the then-known facts. "I think there is a moral to this story," Paul Dirac commented later. "Namely, that it is more important to have beauty in one's equations than to have them fit experiment . . . It seems that if one is working from the point of view of getting beauty in one's equations, and if one has really a sound insight, one is on a sure line of progress."

Sometimes the connection between art and science can be even more direct. Danish physicist Niels Bohr was known for his fascination with cubism—especially "that an object could be several things, could change, could be seen as a face, a limb, and a fruit bowl." He went on to develop his philosophy of complementarity, which showed how an electron could change, could be seen either as a particle or a wave. Like cubism, complementarity allowed contradictory views to coexist in the same natural frame.

Some people wonder how art and science ever got so far separated in the first place. The definitions of both disciplines have narrowed considerably since the days when science was natural philosophy, and art included the work of artisans of the kind who build today's fantastic particle accelerators. "Science acquired its present limited meaning barely before the nineteenth century," writes Sir Geoffrey Vickers in Judith Wechsler's collection of essays *On Aesthetics in Science*. "It came to apply to a method of testing hypotheses about the natural world by observations or experiments. . . ." Surely, this has little to do with art. But Vickers suspects the difference is deeper. People want to believe that science is a rational process, that it is describable. Intuition is not describable, and should therefore be relegated to a place outside the realm of science. "Because our culture has somehow generated the unsupported and improbable belief that everything real must be fully describable, it is unwilling to acknowledge the existence of intuition."

There are, of course, substantial differences between art and science. Science is written in the universal language of mathematics; it is, far more than art, a shared perception of the world. Scientific insights can be tested by the good old scientific method. And scientists have to try to be dispassionate about the conduct of their work—at least enough so that their passions do not disrupt the outcome of experiments. Of course, sometimes they do: "Great thinkers are never passive before the facts," says Stephen Jay Gould. "They have hopes and hunches, and they try hard to construct the world in their light. Hence, great thinkers also make great errors."

But in the end, the connections between art and science may be closer than we think, and they may be rooted most of all in a person's motivations to do art, or science, in the first place. MIT metallurgist Cyril Stanley Smith became interested in the history of his field and was surprised to find that the earliest knowledge about metals and their properties was provided by objects in art museums. "Slowly, I came to see that this was not a coincidence but a consequence of the very nature of discovery, for discovery derives from aesthetically motivated curiosity and is rarely a result of practical purposefulness." ✦

Cole, K. C. (1983). *The Scientific Aesthetic*. New York: Discover Publications, Inc. Reprinted by permission.

OUTLINE BASED ON MARGINAL NOTES

I. Opening quote from physics text to introduce the topic (Feynman)
   A. Feynman rejects the idea that science makes nature ugly
   B. There is both beauty and creativity in science and art, says Feynman
II. What is the relationship between science and art?
   A. There must be a link because so many scientists are also artists
   B. Art and science cover the same ground (examples to illustrate)

      C. Differing approaches: art is emotional, science is logical

      D. But many scientists disagree; they argue that emotion, caring in science is integral to the process.

      E. Examples of scientific passion, including Einstein

  III. The importance of control and creativity in both science and art

      A. Scientists often proceed based on their own "vision of beauty"

      B. Illustrations from science

      C. Aesthetics serves as "a delicate sieve" for science

  IV. Links between art and science can be quite straightforward

[Continue outline on a separate sheet of paper.]

ILLUMINATION AND VERIFICATION

An essential part of your research is the evolution of your understanding of the subject. As you read and evaluate your sources, you will be seeking a solution to your starting question. Several preliminary writing tasks can help you evaluate your sources and understand your topic better.

Evaluation

In your working bibliography, you record the information needed to find a source in the library. Once you have located a source, you need to evaluate it for its usefulness to your particular research project and to your starting question. Every library search will entail the systematic interaction of examination, evaluation, and possibly elimination of material. It is not unusual for an article with a promising title to turn out to be totally irrelevant. Do not be discouraged by dead ends of this sort—they are an accepted and expected part of the library search. You must not hesitate to eliminate irrelevant or unimportant information. As you read each source, consider the following criteria (see also the section on Active Reading).

Evaluative Criteria

1. The relevance of the work to your topic and starting question
2. The timeliness or recency of the work (particularly important in scientific research projects)
3. The author of the work (based on all available information)
4. The prestige or nature of the journal (scholarly or popular press)
5. The controversial nature of the source (whether it agrees with or contradicts other sources)

As you encounter new sources, you will be the best judge of whether or not a particular source contains useful information for your research project. Record your evaluative comments in your research notebook.

WRITING FROM SOURCES

Reading actively and taking accurate and careful notes in the form of paraphrases and summaries are the first important techniques for working with sources. Your reading notes will form the basis for all your subsequent writing about that particular source. In this section, we will discuss three important approaches to source books and articles that result in three different kinds of writing. These are (1) summarizing the main points of the source book or article in condensed form, (2) synthesizing the information found in two or more related sources, and (3) critiquing the information found in one or more sources. These three kinds of writing differ from each other in the approach the writer takes to the source in each instance. Your purpose for writing summaries will be different from your purpose for writing syntheses or critiques. Although the source or subject may remain the same, your approach to that source or subject can change, depending on your purpose. Using different approaches to the same sources will help you to understand those sources better.

Summarizing

When summarizing, the writer takes an entirely objective approach to the subject and the source. The writer of summaries is obliged to accurately record the author's meaning. To do this, of course, the summarizer must first understand the source and identify its key ideas during active reading. Since, in general, a summary is about one third as long as the source itself, this means that two thirds of the information in the original is left out of the summary. So, what do you as summarizer eliminate? Typically, it is the extended examples, illustrations, and explanations of the original that are left out of a summary. The summarizer attempts to abstract only the gist of the piece, its key ideas and its line of argument. If a reader desires more information than that provided in a summary, he or she may look up the original.

To write a summary, first transcribe your short marginal reading notes onto a separate sheet of paper (see the outline on p. 53–54). Read these notes and decide what you think the author's overall point was. Write the main point in the form of a thesis statement that encapsulates the central idea of the whole article.

Thesis: `Cole thinks that there are close connections`
`between science and art that stem from the creative`
`spirit of humanity.`

Be sure not to use the author's words; rather, paraphrase the author's central idea in your own words. Then, by combining the thesis sentence with the marginal notes, you will have constructed the first outline of your summary. Revise the outline for coherence and logical progression of thought.

Next, write the first draft of your summary, following your outline rather than the source. Use your own words, not the words of the author, paraphrasing and condensing his or her ideas. If you want to use the author's own words for a particular passage, use quotation marks to indicate the author's exact words and insert a page reference in parentheses:

`Cole observes that "a tree is fertile ground`
`for both the poet and the botanist" (54).`

In the first few sentences of your summary, introduce the source book or article and its author:

`In the article "The Scientific Aesthetic"`
`(Discover, Dec. 1983, pp. 16-17), the author,`
`K. C. Cole, discusses the relationship of`
`aesthetics and science.`

Follow this context information with the thesis statement, which reflects the author's position, and then with the summary itself. Do not insert your own ideas or opinions into the summary. Your summary should reflect the content of the original as accurately and objectively as possible.

When you have completed the first draft of your summary, review the source to be certain that your draft reflects its content completely and accurately. Then reread your draft to determine whether it is clear, coherent, and concise. Next, revise the summary for style and usage, making your sentences flow smoothly and correcting your grammar and punctuation. Finally, write and proofread the final draft. Remember, your summary will recount objectively and in your own words what someone else wrote, so you should refer often to the author by name.

Synthesizing

When synthesizing, you will approach your material with an eye to finding the relationships among sources. Your purpose will be to discern those relationships and present them coherently and persuasively to your potential readers. Again, the process begins with the active reading of the sources. As you read, highlight and summarize key ideas from your sources in the margins. But instead of simply summarizing the information in one source, look for relationships between ideas in one source and those in another. The sources may be related in one or more of the following ways:

- They may provide examples of a general topic, or one source may serve to exemplify another.
- They may describe or define the topic you are researching.
- They may present information or ideas that can be compared or contrasted.

You must decide in what way or ways your sources are related. When you have decided on the relationships among the sources, write a thesis sentence that embodies that relationship. This thesis sentence should indicate the central idea of your synthesis.

Write an outline of your synthesis paper based on the organizational plan suggested by the thesis statement. This outline should articulate the relationship you have discerned among the sources.

After outlining your synthesis, write the first draft of your paper. In the introductory section of your synthesis, just as in the summary, introduce the sources and their authors. Follow the introduction of sources with your thesis expressing the relationship among the sources. As you write your first draft, keep your thesis in mind, selecting from your sources only the information that develops and supports that thesis. You may want to discuss each source separately, as in the example above, or you may prefer to organize your paper to present major supporting points in the most logical sequence, using information from the sources to develop or support those points. Be sure that you acknowledge all ideas and information from your sources each time you use them in your synthesis.

Upon completion of your first draft, review the sources to be sure you have represented the authors' views fairly and cited source ideas and information properly. Reread your first draft to make sure it is organized logically and that it supports your thesis effectively. Be certain that you have included sufficient transitions between the various sections of your synthesis. Revise your synthesis for style and correctness. Finally, write and proofread the final draft of your synthesis. In general, a synthesis should give the reader a persuasive interpretation of the relationship you have discerned among your sources.

Critiquing

In the third kind of writing from sources, critiquing, the writer takes a critical or evaluative approach to a particular source. When writing critiques, you argue a point that seems important to you based on your own evaluation of the issues and ideas you have encountered in your sources. Critiques are necessarily more difficult to write than summaries or syntheses, because they require that you think critically and come to an independent judgment about a topic. However, critiques are also the most important kind of writing from sources to master, because in many research situations you are asked to formulate your own opinion and critical judgment (as opposed to simply reporting or presenting the information written by others).

As in the other forms of writing from sources, critiquing begins with active reading and careful notetaking from a source. You must first identify the author's main ideas and points before you can evaluate and critique them. Once you understand the source and the issues it addresses, you are in a position to appraise it critically. Analyze the source in one or more of the following ways:

What is said, by whom, and to whom?

How significant are the author's main points and how well are the points made?

What assumptions does the author make that underlie his or her arguments?

What issues has the author overlooked or what evidence has he or she failed to consider?

Are the author's conclusions valid?

How well is the source written (regarding clarity, organization, language)?

What stylistic or rhetorical features affect the source's content?

Other questions may occur to you as you critique the source, but these will serve to get you started in your critical appraisal. To think critically about a source, look behind the arguments themselves to the basis for those arguments. What reasons does the author give for holding a certain belief? In addition, try to discern what assumptions the author is making about the subject. Do you share those assumptions? Are they valid? It is your job to evaluate fairly but with discerning judgment, since this evaluation will be the core of your critique. Formulate a thesis that states your evaluation. Do not feel that your evaluation must necessarily be negative; it is possible to make a positive critique, a negative critique, or a critique that cites both kinds of qualities. Write an outline of your critique, including the following:

1. An introduction of the subject you wish to address and the source article you wish to critique. Be sure to include a complete citation for the source.
2. A statement of your judgment about the issue in the form of a thesis. In that thesis statement, give your own opinion, which will be supported in the critique itself.
3. The body of the critique. First, briefly summarize the source itself. Then review the issues at hand and explain the background facts and assumptions your readers must understand to share your judgment. Use the bulk of your critique (about two thirds) to review the author's position in light of your judgment and evaluation.
4. Your conclusion, which reminds the reader of your main points and the reasons you made them.

After completing your outline, write the first draft of your critique, using your outline as a guide. Make certain that all your points are well supported with specific references to the source. Also, make certain that your main points are related to each other and to the thesis statement.

Review the source to be sure you have represented the author's ideas accurately and fairly. Reread your first draft to determine whether your thesis is clearly stated, your paper logically organized, and your thesis adequately and correctly supported. Revise your critique for content, style, and correctness. Finally, write and proofread the final draft of your critique.

Unfortunately, because critiques are subjective, it is not possible to be any more explicit in guiding your writing of them. The substance of the critique will depend entirely on the judgment you make about the source. Remember, though, that a critique needs to be well supported and your opinion well justified by evidence drawn from the source itself. In the exercises that follow, you will have the opportunity to practice writing summaries, syntheses, and critiques. It will also be valuable to write summaries, syntheses, and critiques of sources you are using in your research project as a way to better understand that topic. Do all such preliminary writing in your research notebook.

✦ EXERCISES

1. *Summary*
   Carefully read, underline, and annotate an article you have encountered in your own research. Using the procedure described above, write a summary of the article. Be certain to turn in to your teacher both your summary and a photocopy of the article you are summarizing.

2. *Synthesis*
   A. Use two or more articles you have encountered in your research as the basis for an extended definition of an important concept. For example, you could write an extended definition of childhood schizophrenia based on the explanations you find in several articles.

   B. Use two or more articles to compare and contrast an idea presented by different authors. Again, using the schizophrenia example, perhaps two or more articles seem to disagree about whether or not a particular treatment is effective. You could write a paper that contrasted their views.

   C. Use the illustrations and examples from two or more articles to describe something. For example, you could write a paper that described several children suffering from particular mental illnesses. For such a paper, you would cite specific cases or examples as reported by the authors, but divide your examples into categories or types of distinguishing characteristics.

3. *Critique*
   Write an evaluative critique of an article you have encountered in your own research. Remember, in a critique it is appropriate to include your opinions and experiences as well as your reactions to the article itself.

4

♦ ♦ ♦

Primary Research Methods: Writing a Research Report

In all disciplines, the primary research methods are the customary ways in which investigators gather information and search for solutions to problems they have posed. For example, when a sociologist conducts a survey, that is primary research, and when an archaeologist goes on a dig, that is also primary research. When conducting primary research, researchers are gathering and analyzing data. Secondary research, in contrast to primary research, involves studying and analyzing the primary research of others as it has been reported in books and journals. So when the sociologist reads the relevant journals in the field and the archaeologist reads topographical maps of the area to be studied, they are doing secondary research. Many research projects are based on a combination of primary and secondary research methods.

PRIMARY RESEARCH IN THE SOCIAL SCIENCES

The social sciences have incorporated many of the research techniques of the natural and physical sciences and have developed some research methods of their own as well. Remember, as we discussed in Chapter 1, the primary aim of the social sciences is to study human beings and their interaction with society and the environment. Social scientists seek to help us understand the events that happen around us and to communicate that understanding to others. Systematic inquiry is essential in the social sciences. Because researchers must communicate the social knowledge they acquire through their research, they need a clear written form for transmitting their insights. As in the natural and physical sciences, researchers in the social sciences employ a version of the scientific method. The following steps (discussed in detail in later paragraphs) are generally utilized in the researching of a social scientific question:

1. Choosing the research problem and stating the hypothesis
2. Formulating the research design and method of gathering data
3. Gathering the data
4. Analyzing the data
5. Interpreting the results of the data analysis in order to test the hypothesis

Step 1—Problem and Hypothesis

Obviously, the first step must be preceded by extensive study and preparation in the discipline under investigation. To choose a research problem that is significant, fresh, and researchable, the social scientist must have an intimate knowledge of the field of study. Often, researchers will choose a problem based on the prior research of other social scientists, or they will seek to test their hypotheses of reality against actual social reality. It is crucial for researchers to keep abreast of the current research in their fields by reading professional journals, attending national meetings of professional societies, and maintaining contacts with other researchers doing similar studies. Research problems are not formulated in a vacuum. The first two inquiry steps discussed in Chapter 1, preparation and incubation, precede the actual formulation of a hypothesis.

Once a significant research problem has been chosen, a working hypothesis can be formulated, that is, the researcher sets forth a proposition (hypothesis) that may explain the occurrence of the phenomenon observed. For example, an education researcher interested in the writing processes of children might hypothesize that the type of learning environment could influence the children's willingness to write.

Step 2—Research Design

The researcher must decide how to test the hypothesis posed in step 1. To do this, he or she needs to determine which concepts or events being studied are constant and which are variable. Variables are phenomena that change or differ. Temperature, for example, is a scientific variable that differs by degrees. Thus, the variable "temperature" contains the idea of more or less heat, and this variable influences the physical world. Similarly, the social variable "religion" may be expressed differently: Protestant, Catholic, Muslim, and so on. Just as temperature influences physical nature, a social variable such as religion influences human nature. Public opinion polls have discovered that Protestants and Catholics differ predictably in their preference for political parties. Thus, the variable "religion" influences social behavior. In the example given from education, the variable is "learning environment," which refers to the formal or informal structure of the classroom—whether open or highly rigid.

Once the variables have been identified, the researcher must decide how best to measure them. The methods used by social scientists include experiments, surveys and questionnaires, interviews and case studies, and observations. These methods are discussed in detail on pp. 65–70.

Step 3—Gathering the Data

The researcher gathers data (both quantitative and qualitative) based on the research design chosen as most appropriate for testing the hypothesis. Social science researchers pay close attention to matters of accurate sampling and the accurate recording of data. Table 4-1 on page 64, taken from FBI Crime Reports, illustrates the kind of data often used by social scientists.

Step 4—Analyzing the Data

Researchers analyze their data quantitatively (using numbers) to discern its relationship to the hypothesis. Depending on the research method used, the researcher relies to a greater or lesser degree on statistical analyses of the data. Often, researchers code their data to make it suitable for computer processing. Computers can quickly and accurately process data and correlate variables. As an example of data analysis, students in a political science class were asked to analyze the crime statistics data in the accompanying Table 4-1. First, the students were asked to compare the data for two states, in this case Alaska and Arizona, to see whether the differences were statistically significant. Then they were asked to explain or interpret their results.

Step 5—Interpreting the Results

The relationship among variables suggested by the hypothesis is tested at this stage in the research, often through statistical measures. In

TABLE 4-1 FBI Uniform Crime Reports

Area	Population	Crime Index Total	Modified Crime Index Total	Violent Crime	Property Crime	Murder and Non-Negligent Manslaughter	Forcible Rape	Robbery	Aggravated Assault	Burglary	Larceny-Theft	Motor Vehicle Theft
ALASKA												
Metropolitan Statistical Area	231,039											
Area actually reporting	100.0%	13,746		1,025	12,721	15	154	285	571	2,113	9,491	1,117
Other Cities	168,591											
Area actually reporting	87.4%	8,100		590	7,510	9	69	62	450	1,081	5,581	848
Estimated totals	100.0%	9,267		675	8,592	10	79	71	515	1,237	6,385	970
Rural	125,370											
Area actually reporting	100.0%	5,219		691	4,528	28	108	28	527	1,743	2,319	466
State Total	525,000	28,232		2,391	25,841	53	341	384	1,613	5,093	18,195	2,553
Rate per 100,000 inhabitants		5,377.5		455.4	4,922.1	10.1	65.0	73.1	307.2	970.1	3,465.7	486.3
ARIZONA												
Metropolitan Statistical Area	2,587,955											
Area actually reporting	100.0%	204,538		17,226	187,312	206	1,208	4,262	11,550	46,196	128,869	12,247
Other Cities	422,312											
Area actually reporting	98.3%	30,282		2,267	28,015	17	139	347	1,764	6,145	20,379	1,491
Estimated totals	100.0%	30,803		2,305	28,498	17	141	353	1,794	6,251	20,730	1,517
Rural	375,733											
Area actually reporting	91.0%	7,342		1,103	6,239	27	43	66	967	2,378	3,366	495
Estimated totals	100.0%	8,064		1,211	6,853	30	47	72	1,062	2,612	3,697	544
State Total	3,386,000	243,405		20,742	222,663	253	1,396	4,687	14,406	55,059	153,296	14,308
Rate per 100,000 inhabitants		7,188.6		612.6	6,576.0	7.5	41.2	138.4	425.5	1,626.1	4,527.3	422.6

the social sciences, a hypothesis can never be proved or disproved "beyond the shadow of a doubt." However, researchers can statistically calculate the probability of error for the hypothesis and thus can strongly suggest the truth or validity of the hypothesis. In other words, a social scientist may be able to either reject or fail to reject a hypothesis based on a careful marshaling of the evidence. For example, in comparing the crime reports for Alaska and Arizona, the students noticed that the rates per 100,000 population differed in potentially interesting ways: Arizona exceeded Alaska in total property crimes (burglary, larceny-theft, motor vehicle theft) and in total violent crimes (murder, rape, robbery, assault). But for individual crimes, Alaska topped Arizona in murders, rapes, and vehicle thefts. The students needed first to find out whether these perceived differences were significant, using statistical tests. If so, they then could interpret their results by positing plausible explanations (hypotheses) to further explore and test. The students, for example, hypothesized that the high number of rapes in Alaska could be related to the scarcity of women. This hypothesis could be tested, perhaps by comparisons with other states with similar demographics.

SOCIAL SCIENCE RESEARCH DESIGNS

The research designs used in social science research include the following:

1. Experiments
2. Surveys and questionnaires
3. Interviews and case studies
4. Observations

Outlined in the paragraphs that follow are the research designs most commonly used by social science researchers. Each has both advantages and disadvantages. Researchers must keep the relative merits in mind as they design a research project.[2]

Experiments

The social scientific experiment is a highly controlled method of determining a direct link between two variables—for example, between high temperature and riots. The researcher must have control over the research environment so that no external variables can affect the outcome. Unlike experimental methods in the sciences, in social scientific research it is often difficult to control the research environment totally.

A researcher who is interested in the causes of riots should not attempt to create a riot in the laboratory for study. However, social science researchers can study laboratory animals and posit hypotheses about human behavior based on their experimental results. For example, to test the hypothesis that overcrowding can cause riots, some researchers studied populations of rats and varied the population density to test their hypothesis. They found that for the rat populations, overcrowding did indeed cause antisocial behavior. From this result, the researchers hypothesized that a similar phenomenon may exist for people—that is, overcrowded cities may contribute to antisocial behavior. Although experimental research is the best means of definitively establishing causal links (variable A causes variable B; overcrowded living conditions cause antisocial behavior), experiments may be limited in applicability. In the case of the above experiment, people may or may not behave as rats do.

Surveys and Questionnaires

Ideally, we would study an entire population to gain insights into its society; finding out how all Americans intend to vote in an upcoming election would accurately predict the outcome. However, polling an entire population is seldom feasible, so pollsters sample small segments of the entire population at random. The most frequently used sampling is random-digit-dialing over the telephone. Researchers have refined sampling techniques to the point that polls can be quite accurate. Thus, CBS news can announce the outcome of a presidential election hours before the returns are in for much of the country.

One particular kind of survey is the questionnaire, a form that asks for responses to a set of questions. Large numbers of people can be polled for their opinions by means of questionnaires over the telephone, through the mail, or in person. The advent of computers has radically changed the survey business: it is now possible to survey large populations, input and code their responses into a computer database, and obtain immediate analyses of the data.

The Hypothesis.   As with most other research in both the sciences and social sciences, the first, and perhaps most important, step in survey research is the articulation of a hypothesis. "Developing the hypothesis provides the key ingredient to structure all subsequent parts of the project: the questionnaire, the sample, the coding, the tabulation forms, and the final report itself."[3] A questionnaire is not given simply to gather random facts; rather, it is a problem-solving enterprise. The researcher poses a hypothesis in an attempt to shed light on a particular research problem. The questionnaire works to either support or counter the hypothesis. For example, in a study of the relationship between the elderly and the police, the researchers presumably would try to solve a problem, for example, that the elderly do not see the police in a positive light and therefore hesitate to call on them in an emergency situation. The researcher, then, might hypothesize that the real problem lies in the elderly population's erroneous perceptions of the police. A questionnaire could be designed to elicit their perceptions and to try to understand the origins of their distrust. In fact, when a study like this was conducted in a major metropolitan area, researchers discovered that an elderly person's distrust of the police was in direct proportion to the number of hours of TV viewed, in particular TV crime shows.

Question Design. The survey researcher must design each question on the questionnaire carefully to ensure that it is clear, direct, and understandable to the target population. Questions should be pre-tested so that initial responses can be reviewed and the questions revised to eliminate any ambiguity prior to their use in the actual study. Researchers should also design questionnaires that are reliable (measure the same thing each time) and valid (measure what they claim to measure). In addition, the population sampled should represent the larger group being studied.

Two basic kinds of questions are used on questionnaires: open-ended questions and closed questions. The open-ended questions may require an interviewer, since research has shown that self-administered open answers tend to yield less usable data. Fowler says that "generally speaking, if one is going to have a self-administered questionnaire, one must reconcile oneself to closed questions, that is, questions that can be answered by simply checking a box or circling the proper response from a set provided by the researcher."[4] On the other hand, Labaw says that open questions have gotten a lot of undeserved bad press in the survey business in recent years. She says they "provide absolutely indispensable insight into how respondents interpret complex but apparently single-issue questions"[5] and, in general, recommends the strategic coupling of both closed and open-ended questions. She also states that "the most basic principle of question wording, and one very often ignored or simply unseen, is that only one concept or issue or meaning should be included in a question."[6]

The accompanying questionnaire was designed by a student to discover the attitude of foreign students toward Utah State University and the education they were receiving. He hypothesized, based on his own experiences as a foreign student, that their responses would be generally very favorable. The student researcher polled sixty foreign students, collected during several visits to the library, representing a variety of nationalities. He found that, in general, foreign students were satisfied with university administrative policies but less satisfied with interpersonal relationships between them and their teachers and classmates.

Questionnaire
1. What is your nationality?
2. How long have you been a student at USU?
3. What is your native language?
4. Do you feel classes at USU are designed with consideration of the needs of foreign students?   yes   no
5. Do you feel your instructors are unbiased toward you and your nationality during class?   yes   no
6. Do you feel you have received an undeserved grade from an instructor due to a bias against foreign students?   yes   no
7. Do you feel any language difficulties (limited vocabulary, accent, etc.) cause communication barriers between you and your instructors?   yes   no
8. Do you feel accepted as an equal by your American classmates?   yes   no
9. Do you feel USU's administrative policies regarding foreign students are fair and unbiased?   yes   no
10. Do you feel USU provides an equal opportunity for a sound education for its foreign students?   yes   no

✦ QUESTIONS FOR DISCUSSION

1. Based on the previous discussion of questionnaire design, how would you rate this student's questionnaire?
2. Do the questions asked match the hypothesis?
3. Are there any ambiguous words or phrases that could be misunderstood?
4. Do you see any way this questionnaire could be made better?

Interviews and Case Studies

Interview studies are one particular type of survey. Their advantages over the questionnaire include flexibility (the questioner can interact with the respondent), response rate (the questioner immediately knows the respondent's answer), and nonverbal behavior (the questioner can gather nonverbal clues as well as verbal). Interviews have other advantages as well, but the disadvantages are also great. Primarily, the time and expense of interviews makes them difficult to conduct. Consequently, fewer responses can be gathered. In addition, the interview is actually a complex interaction between individuals and thus can hinge on the characteristics of the individuals involved. If a respondent is put off by the interviewer, for example, his or her interview answers may be affected. Nevertheless, interviewing is an important research method in the social sciences that results in rich, high-quality data.

Some considerations when designing interviews follow:

1. Be certain that the questions are written down and asked exactly as worded.
2. Be certain that you probe any unclear or incomplete answer.
3. Be certain that inadequate or brief answers are not probed in a biasing (directive) way.

The accompanying interview was conducted by a student who was interested in the relationship between emotions and the onset of asthma attacks in asthmatic children. Prior to the interview, she obtained the subject's permission to tape-record for later data analysis.

Interview with Dr. John W. Carlisle, September 10, 1988
(Pediatrician with extensive experience treating asthmatic children)

1. *Do emotions cause asthma?* Dr. Carlisle feels that the misconception "emotions cause asthma" is easily explained by the fact that stressful emotional situations frequently trigger asthma attacks. People who may have already been prone to asthma may experience their first attack in an emotionally stressful situation. In actuality, asthma is a physical disease that can be irritated by emotional stress or trauma.

2. *What emotional or psychological effects on your asthmatic patients have you observed?* Dr. Carlisle targeted several detrimental effects of asthma on children's emotional and psychological well-being. Older children (8–12 years) feel "defective" in some way because they are suddenly different from their peers (they often have to take medicine or other precautions to prevent an attack). Older children may rebel against parents who expect them to take on the extra responsibility for controlling their own disease. Younger children tend to regress, become very frightened, and cling to parents because they are not yet capable of understanding their disease.

3. *What suggestions do you have for treating the emotional aspects of asthma?* In Dr. Carlisle's opinion, the best emotional support parents can give childhood asthmatics is to make sure they understand the disease and what is happening to them. At the same time, try to reinforce the fact that there will always be someone there to help them if they need help. This can alleviate a great deal of the anxiety that can aggravate their condition.

Observations

The survey method is important for obtaining a person's opinion on a particular issue. The observation, on the other hand, is best suited to the collection of nonverbal data. In this method, the observer takes notes on people behaving in customary ways in a particular environment or setting. In this way, the researcher accumulates "field notes," which are used to analyze trends and discern customary behaviors. The disadvantages of observation include lack of control over the environment, lack of quantifiable data, and small sample size. Also, whenever an observer enters the environment to observe people, the participants' behavior may no longer be natural.

The goal of social research based on observation and description is a general one: to describe and perhaps evaluate a culture or subculture in as much detail as possible. An example of this type of observational research is sociologist Margaret Mead's book *Coming of Age in Samoa*. In this book, Mead describes the complex culture of the Samoan island, paying particular attention to customs surrounding the transition from adolescence to adulthood.

The following excerpt from a report written for a speech communications course illustrates an observation and description of a particular cultural setting—the country singles bar.[7] The researcher was observing particular nonverbal behaviors exhibited by the patrons of the bar. As you read the report, notice the descriptions and categorizations of the patrons in this subculture.

Red Raider Romances

by Lee Guyette

The following study was conducted at
the Red Raider Club in Lubbock, Texas.
The study is a brief survey of the nonverbal communication displayed in this particular club. The following observations were
made by me not only in the recent few days,
but also over a seven-month period in which
I worked as a cocktail waitress there. I
made my observations from the standpoint of
a nonperson/waitress and from the person/
female customer. The Red Raider Club is a
Country and Western club that caters pri-
mar- ily to a crowd of people between the
ages of 25 and 50. It is for the most
part a blue-collar, lower-middle class
crowd.

Body Types, Shapes, and Sizes

Attractiveness

A majority of the people, both male
and female, were only average in appearance. There were a few exceptionally attractive males and females, and they did
seem to get preferential treatment; for example, the attractive men were turned down

less when they asked a woman to dance, and the attractive women were asked to dance more frequently.

Body Image and Appearance

Many of the individuals were slightly overweight. They did not seem to be very aware of or satisfied with their bodies. Their body concept seemed low. In the more attractive individuals, the reverse was true. The attractive individuals were more aware of their bodies; they noticed what they were doing with their bodies, and they smiled more and seemed in general more comfortable with themselves. I did notice that the less attractive people seemed to worry less about their unsightly bodies as they became intoxicated.

Body Messages

Most of my subjects were definitely endomorphic, and they certainly seemed viscerotonic. Most of the men were slightly overweight. There were women as tall as six feet and men as short as five feet. Nearly all my subjects were white. Perhaps two percent were Hispanic and there were no blacks. Many of the men had beards and moustaches, perhaps to indicate masculinity. Most of the women wore their hair either long and curly or short and straight.

Clothing and Personal Artifacts

Function of Dress

The main function of dress in this club was cultural display more than comfort or modesty. Nearly all of the subjects of both sexes wore jeans. The men wore Wranglers and most of the women wore designer jeans. Chic, Lee, Wrangler, Sergio, and Vanderbilt were the most commonly worn for the women. A few women wore western dresses. I did not see any man not wearing cowboy boots and most of the women also wore cowboy boots. A few women wore high-heeled shoes. All of the women wearing dresses wore heels. Most of the people, both female and male, wearing jeans and boots also had their names on the back of their belts. For the men, it was their last names on the belt; for the women, their first names.

Communication Components of Dress

It is difficult to say whether or not these people were intentionally or unintentionally communicating messages through dress. They all seemed to communicate their preference for western dress. They did not wish to communicate, however, that they were from a lower socioeconomic background by wearing western dress. Although this conception has changed in recent years, it still is thought that lower-middle-class people wear western clothes.

Personality Correlates of Dress

It is extremely difficult to assess personality types of a large group just from their clothing styles. However, I did notice that most of the women in dresses were there with dates. I also noticed that women wearing red western blouses danced more frequently. For the most part, both men and women dressed conservatively. The colors were usually solid black, brown, and white for the men, and red, purple, or blue for the women.

Perception of Dress

Most of the people were dressed in the conventional stereotype of western dress. Indeed, it was almost as if there were an unspoken dress code. The young attractive girls, wearing red and purple blouses with ruffles, tight jeans, boots, belts, and wearing their hair long, seemed to be thought the sexiest and most likeable. They were asked to dance more frequently than any others. The young attractive men with beards and moustaches wearing black or white western cut shirts seemed to be the most popular with the women. No one wore

very much jewelry of any kind. A few women
had small earrings or hair barrettes.
Nearly everyone smoked cigarettes continu-
ously. I saw no pipes or cigars.

The Effects of Dress
        The main effect I observed was that
everyone seemed able to identify with each
other and feel a sense of belonging to the
group because of their similar style of
dress.

[Researcher goes on to describe behaviors observed according to the following categories: body movements and ges-
tures; facial expressions and eye behavior; responses to
environment; personal space, territory, and crowding;
touching behavior; voice characteristics; taste and smell;
culture and time.]

Discussion
        I feel that the nonverbal communica-
tion that I have described may be representative of lower-middle-class America in
Lubbock, Texas. The nonverbal communication
described in this report may illustrate
lower-middle-class values: the tendency to
be slightly overweight in both sexes; the
conservative, traditional, western-style
dress; the traditional use of male/female
regulators and posture; the overcontrol of
masculine expressions of emotion and the
lack of control in feminine emotional expressions; the environment, with its tacky

chairs and dirty carpet; the use of territory by the men; the fact that women have
no true territory, personal space, or value
(the women are treated as possessions and
property and they have only as much value
as they are granted by men); the way in
which the men have absolute control over
when and how they will be touched, but the
women have very little to say about when or
how the men will touch them; the way the
women plead with soft cooing pitch at the
end of their voice or
remain silent while the men speak loudly
and uninterruptedly; the use of substandard
speech; the accepted deception on the part
of the males; the overwhelming smell of to-
bacco and liquor and stale urine in the re-
strooms; the taste of cheap wines, beer,
and whisky; the time being measured by the
sets the band plays. All of these things
are often associated with lower-middle
classes. Women and men may be poorly educated and thus rely on tradition and myth.
I felt that the nonverbal communication
that I observed was representative of this
particular subculture.

✦ QUESTIONS FOR DISCUSSION

1. What is the relationship between the observer and those she is observing?

2. Observation research tends to both describe and classify behaviors of individuals in order to predict future behaviors within the setting. List the classifications used by this writer. Do they seem appropriate to the behaviors observed? Why or why not?

3. Does the writer overgeneralize from a small sample; that is, does she jump to conclusions based on insufficient data? Why or why not? Do her conclusions follow logically from her evidence? Why or why not?

4. Is it likely that the observer's presence changed the dynamics of the situation so that her subjects' behavior was no longer natural? Why or why not?

5. Do the writer's personal opinions and biases come through? Why or why not?

6. How much can an observer infer about the subjects' thoughts and emotions from observing their behaviors? For example, in the subsection "Communication Components of Dress," the author states that "they did not wish to communicate, however, that they were from a lower socioeconomic background. . . ." Is this a valid inference or a reflection of a personal bias? Justify your response.

✦ EXERCISES

The exercises below are provided to give you an opportunity to try out some of the primary research techniques frequently used by social scientists. Or, you may wish to adapt these methods to find information pertinent to your own research topic with an eye toward incorporating the primary research data you discover into your larger research paper.

1. To understand observing and reporting, begin by observing the behavior of a particular group or subculture and report on that observation. You may find that an observation report would be a helpful component in a larger research paper project. As in the sample paper above on the country singles bar, first choose subjects in a "field" to observe. Some possibilities include customers at a fast-food restaurant, patrons at a theater, participants in a

sport, spectators at a rock concert, students in a dorm, customers in a department store elevator, and so on.

Procedure:

A. Identify the field you have chosen to observe. Describe the setting, location, and the time you spent observing. Describe your research method. (Are you an observer or participant?)

B. Take field notes as you observe the behaviors of the individuals in your chosen group. Look for verbal and nonverbal behaviors.

C. Categorize your field notes into related behaviors and personality types.

D. Speculate on the meaning of the behaviors you observed. What did you learn about the people in your study and how they act? Give possible reasons for why they behaved as they did.

E. Write up your field observations in a report three to five pages long.

2. To understand the processes of interviewing and reporting, conduct an actual interview, working by yourself or with a classmate. You may find that an interview with an expert is a useful component of a larger research paper project.

Procedure:

A. Find someone in your intended major field. Write or phone the person to introduce yourself. Set up an interview with that person, explaining that you want to find out what a person in your chosen career actually does.

B. Prior to the interview, draw up a list of interview topics similar to the following:

- education and background
- job title and general description of the job
- description of the company or organization
- years at the job
- prior positions within the same company
- tasks performed in the job
- tools used in the job (for example, computers, books)
- career plans or aspirations
- job satisfaction
- advice for someone just beginning in the field

Use this topic list as a model only in developing your questions. The questions you ask will vary in accordance with your career choice. It is important to think through the questions you intend to ask your informant very carefully. If you want to tape the interview, be certain to ask for permission.

C. Once you have collected your data, analyze and categorize it into a report three to five pages long. Someone reading your report should be able to discern what the career is like for participants.

FIELD OBSERVATION AND REPORTS

The study reported on below illustrates one of two main types of writing done by social scientists—the research report. (The other major type of writing is the review paper, discussed in Chapter 6.)

In research reports, social scientists describe in detail research that they themselves have conducted to share their findings with the scientific world in general and thus advance knowledge in their field. Because it is important that social scientists be able to replicate each other's research, a customary format for organizing research reports has been developed that can be easily recognized by all social scientists.

The standard research report format follows the scientific method that was discussed on p. 63. The parts generally found in the research report are Title, Abstract or Summary, Introduction, Materials and Methods, Results, Discussion and Conclusions, and Literature or Works Cited. They correspond generally to the scientific method:

1. The researcher formulates a question and develops a hypothesis that might possibly answer the question posed. [The hypothesis is typically posed in the research report *Introduction*.]
2. On the basis of the hypothesis, the researcher predicts what should be observed under specified conditions and circumstances. [The prediction of expectations is typically posed in the research report *Introduction*.]
3. The researcher makes the necessary observations, generally using carefully designed, controlled experiments. [The detailed description of the experiment is included in the *Materials and Methods* section of the research report.]
4. The researcher either accepts or rejects the hypothesis depending on whether or not the actual observations corresponded with the predicted observations. [The scientist's decision to accept or reject the hypothesis is generally included in the *Results* section of the

research report. This section is typically followed by a *Discussion and Conclusion* section that interprets results for the readers.]

When writing your research report, you will not necessarily write it in the order that it finally appears. In fact, you may find it easiest to write the Materials and Methods section first, since it is here that you will describe in detail the experiment itself. The Discussion and Conclusion section is probably best written near the end, after you know exactly what you want to say in your Results section. Other parts, like the Abstract and the Works Cited, can be incorporated near the end of your drafting process. Any primary data may be included in one or more appendices, included immediately after the works cited list.

The following paper by an anthropology student illustrates a report of an ethnographic study, conducted for an advanced anthropology course.[8] Notice the subheadings that clearly divide the paper into its relevant sections. The references follow the APA format typically used in the social sciences.

Traveling on the Bowlertown Underground:

The Formation of a Lesbian Community

Tamara Pope Roghaar

ANTHROPOLOGY 480

Dr. David Lancy

May 18, 1995

Introduction

Much of the literature on gay communities is focused on men. Although some previous research has been done on lesbian communities, most of it focuses on cities where there are bars and other institutionalized meeting places from which the community is built (Franzen, 1993; Lockard, 1986; Weston, 1991). This study focuses on the lesbian community in a city with a weak institutional base that has developed alternate means of developing and maintaining the lesbian community.

The lesbian community is very well hidden in Bowlertown[1] due to the town's

[1] In this particular community, "Bowler" is a term used by lesbians to refer to other lesbians. It began as a cover term that could be used in the presence of straight people without giving away a person's identity as a lesbian. For example, a woman could describe someone as a bowler and other lesbians would understand that to mean the woman was a lesbian, and any straight people present would not understand the full meaning of the term.

size and political climate. There is only
one readily visible institutionalized
group, the Gay and Lesbian Alliance (GLA),
which advertises its weekly meeting in the
local university newspaper. GLA serves as a
support group for the local gay community,
although lesbian participation is quite
weak. Other than GLA, there are no institutionalized groups or activities in Bowlertown that are visible to the mainstream
community. This paper examines how the lesbian community is formed and maintained in
such a situation. More specifically, this
study examines ways of entering the community, what activities serve as community
maintenance, how the community is struc-
tured, and how members regard the community. The lesbian community in Bowlertown
may be illustrative of the workings of gay
communities in smaller, conservative parts
of the country, unlike places such as San
Francisco or Greenwich Village with a well-
established and somewhat accepted gay
community.

The reference to community in this
paper does not refer to the traditional definition of a community—one that is defined
by geographical boundaries. Rather, it

refers to the community often described in the research—a community based on homosexual collectivity. As Evelyn Hooker stated,

If one is permitted to use the term [community] to refer to an aggregate of persons engaging in common activities, sharing common interests, and having a feeling of socio-psychological unity with variations in the degree to which persons have these characteristics . . . then it is completely germane to homosexuals. (1961, p. 43)

Lockard (1986) specifically defines a lesbian community by four features. First, the community consists of social networks based on shared sexual preference. Secondly, these networks lead to shared group identity or, as Hooker describes it, a socio-psychological unity. The third feature includes shared values and norms, and the fourth is an institutional base (Lockard, 1986). The situation in Bowlertown fits Hooker's definition, as well as Lockard's, if GLA is regarded as the institutional base. Lockard argues that without an institutional base, social networks occur, but not communities. These institu-

tional bases serve two purposes: continuity
through time that is not reliant upon certain individuals and access for new members. The situation in Bowlertown is very
characteristic of Lockard's social network
in that it is reliant upon a network of
friends and participation of individual
members, and these fluctuate and change
through time. On the other hand, GLA does
serve as an institutional base in the sense
that it provides access to the gay community for new members. For the purposes of
this paper, Bowlertown's group will be referred to as a community with the recognition that it has a weak institutional base.

Methodology

All of the women interviewed for this
study were previously acquainted with the
researcher. Although not actively researching at the time, I had attended parties and
activities, visited homes, and had been introduced to other women. Based on this interaction and considerable time spent with
a couple of the women, I was able to learn
about the community and its workings. I
used this background knowledge to form my
research design and areas of focus.

Semi-structured tape recorded interviews were conducted with seven women over
the course of six weeks. I used a grand
tour question (Fetterman, 1989) of "Tell me
about the lesbian community in Bowlertown,"
and the interview would follow from there.
Interviews would last from just under an
hour to two hours. Along with the interviews, my interaction with the women was
maintained.

Because of the special situation that
stigmatization of members of the gay community produces (Warren, 1997), several steps
were taken to conceal the identity of the
women. All names have been changed, and any
other indications of identity have been al-
tered, including the name of the town.
Tapes of the interviews and references in
my notes refer to the pseudonyms of the
women.

All seven of the women that were interviewed were Caucasian and middle class.
Five were either attending, or had gradu-
ated, from the local university. The resul-
tant sample bias is recognized and this
study does not address issues regarding experiences of women from other races or social backgrounds. The women were between

the ages of 19 and 30. The women interviewed represented a fair range of participation in, and identification with, the
lesbian community in Bowlertown. Two women
were very aware of the workings of the community and their role in it, another didn't
feel she was strongly involved in it, and
the other four women's involvement could be
considered moderate and typical. All were
very willing to be interviewed and helped
me a great deal. The seven women interviewed, and another woman mentioned often
by those interviewed, were given a copy of
the rough draft to provide a member check
(Lancy, 1993) in order to verify my interpretations and provide a more accurate,
emic perspective.

The Mainstream Community

A brief introduction to Bowlertown is
necessary to better understand the context
in which the lesbian underground has been
formed. Bowlertown is a small, urban, university town. The city of Bowlertown has a
population of about 33,000 and the surrounding county has a population of about
70,000. 100% of Bowlertown is urban, 79% of
the county is urban. The local university

had an enrollment of 9,200 in 1990. Bowlertown is mostly Caucasian, only 5% of the
county population is non-white. Bowlertown's median household income is just over
$20,000 (U.S. Bureau of the Census, 1990).
85.5% of the county's population are members of the Church of Jesus Christ of Latter Day Saints (Bradley, 1990). The LDS
church's stand on homosexuality is consistently negative. Homosexual members used to
be excommunicated, but now are generally
asked to remain celibate, otherwise regarded as sinners. Non-procreative sex is
seen as the antithesis of the church's doc-
trine that couples should produce the maxi-
mum number of children they are physically
and materially able to care for.

Conservative politics and traditional
values run deep in Bowlertown. Local controversies still are sparked when the gay
community is visible, for example, when the
GLA participated in the University homecom-
ing parade, or at a local gay pride day
gathering. Many of the women interviewed
stated that anything more visible than GLA
would be regarded by the local community
with contempt or even violence. "If they
had a gay bar in Bowlertown it would be

burnt to the ground. There would never be a gay bar in Bowlertown. You'd have people hanging out outside the bar waiting to beat you up when you came out, you know?" Bowlertown's small population also creates a problem. "It's too small of a community, everyone would be pegged, you know? Bloomington's so big that when I was in high school I could go to the bars and my parents wouldn't hear about it because there's a million people in the valley. But in Bowlertown, you know, it's amazing. . . ." Such stigma is placed on homosexuality in Bowlertown that secrecy and anonymity are felt to be quite necessary.

Entry

Because the lesbian community in Bowlertown is so well hidden, entry into it is problematic. The most assured entry is through friends and acquaintances. "Well, once you meet someone who knows someone else and get invited to a party, then you're in a group." Or simply, "Well, once you get invited to a party. . . ." All of the women interviewed for this study entered the community in this way and mentioned this as the easiest way to get into

the community. This creates a problem for
women who are new to the area or who don't
know anyone in the community. GLA then becomes a way to access the community.

Since announcements of weekly meetings
are printed in the student newspaper, a new
member of the community has a way of entering without knowing any specific individuals. This presents a double-edged sword for
those who need to keep closeted, yet need
to find a community. Fears of getting
"caught" going to GLA are the stuff of leg-
ends. Susan told me there was a kind of
running joke about women pacing the halls
the first three or four times before actually making it into the meeting. At the
time of this study, GLA was attended mostly
by men, and the only women that attended
did so because they wanted to be available
for new members of the community. "We've
been going to GLA quite a bit lately, even
though we're the only women there, because
occasionally a woman will come in kind of
in a panic that needs support, needs to
find a community."

GLA serves as a support group, especially for those who have just come out.
Its availability is most important for

those that are new to the area, or who
don't know anybody in the community. Once
social connections are made, GLA fades in
importance. "Like after you've gone to GLA
for a couple of years, and you're kind of
out, you don't need it anymore. It's like
you know other people and you hang out with
them on social occasions, and you don't
need to go to GLA anymore."

When asked about other ways of entering the community, every woman mentioned
softball. This seemed to be a very important event that brought the community together and brought "new blood to the
family, so to speak", as Meg stated. Kate
agreed, "I think athletics is the big way
to get to know other lesbians. Because
like, Andrea for instance, she met all
those baby-dykes,[2] like Heidi and Anna, and
Denise I think is her name, through softball and stuff. And I think they just saw
something in her that was in them." Since
softball season is in the summer, Robin
felt like she was more involved in the com-

---

[2]A baby-dyke is either a very young woman
(still a teenager, usually), or a woman
that doesn't know she's a lesbian yet, but
other lesbians feel she is, or both.

munity in the summer than in the winter,
"Yeah, during the summer it seems like we
hang out more in Bowlertown during the summer than we do in the winter. Cause we play
softball together during the summer, we go
camping . . . during the winter we don't
see each other as much." Softball seemed a
much more accepted and respected entry into
the community than GLA. Comments like,
"Well, you could go to GLA and get right
in, but I wouldn't do that," expressed this
ambivalence.

An important spin-off from entering
the community through certain people and
activities is that of the "mother" role.
Kate told me about a motherly type: "There
was a woman that lived here . . . little
baby-dykes from all over the place were
flocking to her house and just hanging out.
And, I was one of those, and we didn't feel
comfortable at GLA, cause what the hell did
they do there? We just didn't know." Although this particular woman wasn't in the
area anymore, many agreed that Andrea now
filled this role. Such women seem to have
an uncanny way of attracting either young
or closeted women, and by doing so, bring
them into the social network. As Susan

said, "It seems like people just coming out just sort of find her. She feels safe." These women provide a safe and comfortable social setting, often to women who can't name why they seek her out or why it is they feel safe with her. Such a motherly type provides an important way of entering the community, especially for younger, locally raised women.

After a woman has been introduced into the community, she's given a probationary period, or trial time. One woman told me she felt like she had to "prove herself" to them in order to be accepted.[3] Another explained that with new women, especially the young ones, you had to be careful because you never knew who had the big mouth. She explained that if a woman was teaching at a local school, and a girl from that school showed up at a party, the woman teaching may lose her job if that girl had a big mouth. So, although a woman may be introduced to certain members of the community,

[3]This woman was not of the seven officially interviewed, but felt she was part of the community at one point, but not of late since she was dating a man. Some women commented that they never felt like she was part of their community, even when she was dating women.

it does not guarantee that she will be accepted into the community. After one woman tested my trustworthiness, she introduced me by saying, "She's married, but she's O.K."

Entry into the Bowlertown lesbian community, then, is best obtained casually, through friendships, individuals, and specific activities. These include friendship networks, motherly types, softball, and GLA.

Rituals

Zanden (1987) argues that cohesiveness of groups is fostered by a "consciousness of oneness" (p. 404), a recognition by the members of a group that they are not merely in a group, but of a group. This consciousness is enhanced and maintained by the use of rituals: "social acts of symbolic significance that are performed on certain occasions by prescribed tradition" (p. 410). If Zanden's theory is applied to the lesbian community in Bowlertown, then there should be rituals that enhance the community's consciousness of oneness. In large cities, such a meeting place where consciousness-raising rituals take place is

often in the form of a gay bar or other
gay-identified establishments (Achilles,
1964). With the absence of these established meeting places in Bowlertown, it
should be expected that other rituals have
evolved to fill this gap.

During my research, examples of activities or settings which kept the community
together, or rituals, began to emerge. The
primary function of these rituals is to
create social cohesion and a feeling of
"we-ness," unlike gay men's functions which
often serve only as leisurely and sociabil-
ity outlets (Warren, 1974). The women recognized the need to have unifying occasions
and events. "I think we just kind of need
each other and so like in weird ways we
just stay together, like Jill's parties.
Even if its only three times a year." It is
also recognized that Bowlertown lesbian social functions are different from gay
men's, "I think because we have such different cultures. Like gay men are really
into the bar scene, a lot of lesbians are
too, but just have different tastes in what
we like. Like at Jill's house, my God, we
drink coffee, have a couple beers and talk,
and the guys, when they have a party,

they're more into, well, seeing who looks good, and that's just not how we are."

Achilles (1964) argues that bars were adopted as an institution in the homosexual community for several reasons. Most important is that bars cater to a sociable and leisurely activity. Bars are also flexible and mobile, which is necessary due to pressure from law enforcement. Achilles also argues that bars provide some degree of anonymity and segregation from the larger society (1964). With the unavailability of such bars in Bowlertown, different events take place that provide such a setting, perhaps even to a greater extent. Events such as Jill's parties provide a sociable and leisurely environment in addition to being "needed." A "home base" such as Jill's house would be even more flexible, mobile, anonymous, and segregated from the larger society than a bar, a characteristic arguably necessary in Bowlertown. Places such as Jill's can be seen as informal, small town equivalents to a gay bar in a larger city. It is one of the foundations from which the community is built. When referring to one of Jill's parties, Susan said, "That is our community. That's probably more representative [of our community], and you've been there, that is what we're like." Because such informal gatherings are a large part of their cohesive base, shifts in location and individuals occur all of the time. Before Jill's parties were the main meeting place, the "home base" was somewhere else, "At that time, parties were held on every Thursday at the White House. And it was what we called Family Home Evening.[4] A lot of us were failed Mormons, so that was kind of a double pun on family. . . . The White House kind of held us all together, it was a place to meet."

At the time of this study, a few women mentioned that just as the center of activity had shifted from the White House to Jill's, there seemed to be another shift occurring now. "Right now there's a big hole . . . the center has shifted somewhere else. For a while the White House, then up to Jill's, and now it's not there yet. It's not there, it's somewhere else, and maybe—it's like whenever one place goes under,

[4]Family Home Evening is a common activity among practicing Mormons in which the family spends an evening together every week, often in accordance with a spiritual message and prayer.

another one steps up and takes its place,
but it hasn't happened yet, to my knowledge." Another woman explained that the
crowd at Jill's was too young, and another
woman then pointed out how careful you have
to be around the young crowd. Perhaps the
coming out group requires a ritual such as
a party at Jill's house when first coming
out. Then, after they have found their own
groups, the ritual fades in importance,
just as GLA does.

Besides a common meeting place, other
rituals that kept the community together
that were mentioned were shared activities
and interests. Softball was of most importance, all but one woman played softball
every year. The one that didn't play attended games to watch her partner. Softball
brings the community together during the
week via games and practices, and during
the weekends for tournaments and away
games. Softball is a way to bring lesbians
"out of the woodwork" to be reunited, and
for new ones to be introduced. Many other
less formalized activities such as camping,
barbecuing, watching videos, etc. serve as
cohesive rituals. Such activities reflect
an aspect of Lockard's third feature of a

lesbian community, shared values and norms, since "it is the community which provides the means and the settings in which the values and norms of the subculture are learned, shared, and expressed as the visible 'on the ground' behavior and activities of individuals" (p. 86). Activities such as camping, softball, etc. provide a setting in which the shared values and norms of a community are learned. Not only do they function as a gathering place, but also a means of learning the subculture, learning how to become part of the Bowlertown lesbian community.

Segregation

The structure of the Bowlertown lesbian community can be well illustrated by how the community segregates itself. Segregation is not uncommon in lesbian communities (Franzen, 1993; Lockard, 1986). The most important bases for separation in the Bowlertown community seemed to be age and degree of "outness." Other factors included "partying," stereotypical types of lesbians, activities, and shared interests.

Age is a very important basis of segregation in the Bowlertown community. Com-

ments about older lesbians "disappearing"
and "dropping off the edge of the earth"
were common. Some of the older lesbians
won't even acknowledge the younger ones in
public places: "Another aspect of the community, there's a split somewhere, a lot of
the older lesbians that were out for a
while are no longer visible, we don't know
where they are. They're here in the valley,
we see them in the grocery store . . . [but]
they won't even look at us at the grocery
store. . . . It's frustrating to me [that]
they're afraid of being out because we need
to see heroes, we need to see
people . . . that have made it."

In Lockard's (1986) study, age was
also an important basis of segregation.
Older lesbians were reluctant to associate
with the community because of the risk of
losing their jobs through association with
a known lesbian community, and some of them
because of their fear and caution learned
in the years before gay liberation. Andrea's description reflects that reluctance
to be out by some older lesbians, "There's
a group in Bowlertown called the OWLS,
which is the 'older, wiser lesbians,' they
call themselves . . . they're a pretty

tight-knit group, but yet they're all kind
of not out." Such a group is inaccessible
to the larger lesbian community. "They
might have their own, in fact I'm sure they
do, have their own little social
clique . . . But I have no idea how to get
into that. I think they see us younger ones
as like, so out, or too outspoken, or too
controversial kinda."

Meg's earlier comment regarding caution around younger lesbians, using the
high school teacher as an example, illustrates the importance of protecting one's
job. Other comments show more of the same:
"This is what happens, they graduate and
either get a teaching position and have to
shut up—or they move." "They get jobs and
then they just hide." Or, "You get in trouble, I mean, you've got to protect your
job. . . ." Meg also mentioned that older
and younger lesbians just naturally divide
themselves based on shared interests and
activities. Younger, single lesbians seem
to enjoy the bar scene and partying more
than older, "married" lesbians. Meg herself
was getting older and had been with her
partner for nearly seven years, and felt
job protection and different interests were

what kept her and her partner from being
more a part of the community.

Degree of "outness" also seems to be a
basis for segregation. One woman commented
that she wouldn't hang out with the kind of
women that went to GLA. Kate and Susan acknowledged that some gay women might not
want to be seen with them because they look
stereotypically lesbian. A woman whose appearance classifies her as a "hard-core,"
"diesel dyke," or "leather dyke" may be
threatening to more conservatively dressed
gay women, and association with such hard-
core women may label other women. Perhaps
Robin said it most succinctly, "It makes me
sound like a bitch, but I don't want to be
walking down the street and they say, God,
look at the fucking dyke. . . . When you
see those diesel dykes walking down the
road you know, anybody could take one look
at them and know." When asked what a diesel
dyke was, Robin answered, "Well, a big dyke
walking around in their skin tight 501's
and their tennis shoes and their skin
tight, tucked in T-shirt, no bra, with
their hair buzzed about this far over their
ears. . . ." Two Bowlertown lesbians acknowledged that even though they were "the

outest ones [we] know," there were "people
that make [us] uncomfortable . . . they're
so out that they're like, well, they shave
their heads, and wear nose-rings and parade
with T-shirts all the time."

Although age and outness were the most
obvious dividers within the community,
there were smaller, more subtle divisions.
Many women referred to "cliques" and
"groups." Much of the division was based
upon interests and activities, i.e., the
softball crowd. There is a distinction between "butch" and more feminine, "lipstick
lesbians." A butch woman will look stereotypically lesbian, with short hair and masculine or casual clothing. A lipstick
lesbian looks more feminine, wearing makeup
and fashionable clothing. One woman commented that she liked butch lesbians because they were more "real" and "together,"
as they had nothing to hide. Others expressed ambivalence towards "wanna-be, I
don't know what, wanna-be femmes, I guess."
A gay bar in a nearby city is known for
it's "lipstick lesbian" clientele. One such
woman told me that she doesn't date "butch"
women. Other divisions occur between women
that "party" (drink alcohol and do some oc-

casional drugs) and women who don't, between women who enjoy the bar scene and
women who don't, and between women in long-
term relationships and women who tend to
skip around.

Family

Despite these divisions, there is
clearly a shared identity among members of
the lesbian community in Bowlertown. Many
women identify other lesbians as "family."
For example, when speaking of another
woman, they will comment "she's family" to
let other gay women know she's gay. Weston's (1991) research illustrates how many
gay people create "gay families" that are
distinct from their biological families,
but in some ways serve the same function.
Many women in Bowlertown feel they have
created another kind of family in the gay
community, although there is variation in
how important this alternative family is
for different women. When asked why lesbians refer to one another as family, one
woman stated, "because they are. For some
of us they're the only family we've got."
Another said, "When you see someone, you
have a sense of belonging. When you see

someone that you don't even know . . . it feels right, I feel like I've seen some family." Many women talked of specific times when they would turn to their "gay family" before their biological family for help, "If I were in trouble, I don't know if I would go to my [biological] family first." The occurrence of relationship and emotional problems were often mentioned as times when you couldn't turn to your biological family. "The thing that makes me sad is there are times when I want to talk to my mom for advice and things like that, and it's not . . . a possibility." Because of the shared identity and experiences they have with other lesbians, they were often the ones they turned to for support, because "they know what you're going through."

This sense of family can be observed at gatherings such as Jill's parties. Such a gathering is not just a place to get together and socialize, but a definite consciousness of oneness is observable. This realization of common identity and sympathetic identification with other members in the group is directly tied to the degree of cohesiveness in the group (Zanden, 1987).

These parties and other gatherings serve to reinforce this common identity, thus keeping the group together. Much of the talk at Jill's parties circulates around the shared experiences that gay women have in the local culture. Stories regarding family reactions, work situations, and unaccepting Mormons are common. Such experiences are shared by the members of the community, and not by others outside of the community, reinforcing the sense of "we-ness" (Zanden, 1987, p. 404) or cohesiveness. As an observer, I've noted this element is missing from heterosexual parties and bars, whereas its existence is strongly apparent at gay parties and bars.

Conclusion

Although the small town size and conservative political climate in Bowlertown hinders the growth of a stronger institutional base, this paper demonstrates how the lesbian community has developed and how it has maintained itself. This study is illustrative of how a gay community develops before gay bars or other like institutions develop, and may reflect the situation throughout the U.S. before the days of gay liberation. D'Emilio (1983) documents a social environment similar to the one in Bowlertown in the early 20th century. Like Bowlertown, where networks are developed casually, based upon acquaintances, friendships, and activities, so too was the American gay subculture. D'Emilio states,

> Gradually finding methods of meeting one another, these men and women staked out urban spaces and patronized institutions that fostered a group life . . . [they] planned private entertainments that sustained friendships and promised dependable social interaction . . . By 1915, one observer of male homosexual life was already referring to it as "a community distinctly organized." Meeting places for public liaisons, institutions such as bars, and friendship networks dotted the urban landscape."
> (p. 12)

The lesbian community in Bowlertown, then, can be likened to the subculture across the country before a strong institutional base was built. Entry into this world is reliant upon friendships, individuals, and specific activities. Examples of these include friendship networks, motherly types, softball, and GLA. Upon entering the community, cohesiveness is maintained and values and norms learned through rituals such as softball and parties. The community then structures itself, basing its divisions on interests and activities, age, and degree of "outness." Despite the differential structure of the community, a consciousness of oneness and feeling of "we-ness" is maintained.

The lack of a strong institutional base dictates that the lesbian community in Bowlertown is fluid and ever-changing, reliant upon participation of certain individuals and the development of common meeting places. This fluidity is probably enhanced because Bowlertown is basically a college town, where people are moving in and out of town all of the time based on their participation in the university. Despite the fluidity and changing character of Bowlertown's lesbian community, it somehow maintains itself and is accessible to new members. Although well hidden from the mainstream society, its existence is well founded and permanent. Using Bowlertown as an example, the study of community development and maintenance can be enhanced, and an illustration of how lesbian communities form in smaller, more conservative parts of the country is presented. Knowledge of this type of community is needed, as well as the already existing studies done in larger cities with a strong institutional base, in order to better understand the foundations and maintenance of lesbian communities.

References

Achilles, N. (1964). The development of the homosexual bar as an institution. In W. R. Dynes and D. Donaldson (Eds.), Studies in homosexuality: Sociology of homosexuality (pp. 2-18). New York: Garland.

Bradley, M. B. (Ed.). (1990). Churches and church in the United States. Atlanta: Glenmary Research Center.

Fetterman, D. M. (1989). Ethnography: Step by step. Applied social research methods series (V.17). Newbury Park, CA: Sage.

Franzen, T. (1993). Differences and identities: Feminism and the Albuquerque Lesbian community. Signs: Journal of Women in Culture and Society, 18, 891-906.

Hooker, E. (1961). The homosexual community. Proceedings of the XLV international congress of applied psychology, Copenhagen. Berkeley, CA: University of California Press.

Lancy, D. F. (1993). Qualitative research in education: An introduction to the major traditions. New York: Longman.

Lockard, D. (1986). The Lesbian community:
An anthropological approach. In R.
Blackwood, (Ed.), The many faces of
homosexuality: Anthropological
approaches to homosexual behavior
(pp. 316-326). New York: Harrington
Park Press.

U.S. Bureau of the Census: Utah. (1990).
Census demographic information: 1990
state and county social statistics.
Washington, DC: U.S. Government Printing Office.

Warren, C. A. B. (1974). Identity and community in the gay world. New York:
John Wiley & Sons.

Warren, C. A. B. (1977). Fieldwork in the
gay world: Issues in phenomenological
research. Journal of Social Issues,
33, 93-107.

Weston, K. (1991). Families we choose:
Lesbians, gays, kinship. New York:
Columbia University Press.

Zanden, J. W. V. (1987). Social
psychology. New York: Random House.

NOTES

1. This chapter is not intended to be comprehensive, but rather serves as an overview to the types of primary research typical in social sciences. Students desiring more in-depth information should consult one of the many comprehensive guides to social science research methods.

2. Information for this section of the chapter is adapted and reprinted with the permission of The Free Press, a Division of Macmillan, Inc., from *Methods of Social Research*, 2nd ed., by Kenneth D. Bailey. Copyright 1982 by The Free Press.

3. Patricia Labaw, *Advanced Questionnaire Design*. Cambridge, Mass.: ABT Books, 1981; 35.

4. Floyd J. Fowler, Jr. *Survey Research Methods*, 2nd ed. Newberry Park, CA: Sage Publications, 1993; 57.

5. Labaw, p. 134.

6. Labaw, p. 154.

7. I am indebted to Professor John Deethardt of the Texas Tech University Speech Communications Department for passing on to me this assignment and student response.

8. I am indebted to Professor David Lancy of the Utah State University Anthropology Department for passing on to me this student paper.

5

✦ ✦ ✦

Planning, Writing, and Revising Your Research Paper

After you have completed the primary research, library research, and preliminary writing on your topic, you are ready to begin planning the actual research paper. You should consider carefully the following two important components as you begin to plan: rhetorical situation and organization.

RHETORICAL SITUATION

The context in which you are writing an assignment is called the rhetorical situation. The term rhetoric refers to written or spoken communication that seeks to inform someone of something or to convince someone of a particular opinion or point of view. For any writing assignment, you need to analyze the components of the rhetorical situation: (1) the writer's purpose, (2) the writer's persona, (3) the potential readers or audience, (4) the subject matter, and (5) the appropriate language or tone.

Purpose

When preparing to write, a writer must decide on the actual purpose of the piece. What is the goal that should be accomplished? Many times the goal or purpose is implicit in the writing task itself. For example, for a newspaper reporter, the goal is to present the facts in an objective manner, describing events for newspaper readers. For your research paper assignment, you need to determine your purpose or goal and define it carefully. The purpose does not have to be grandiose or profound—it may simply be to convince your readers that you have a fine grasp on the topic and are making some important points, or it may be to inform your readers of the current state of knowledge in a particular field. Kauleen's purpose statement read as follows: "My purpose in this paper is to tell readers who may know nothing about acupuncture in an informative manner how this ancient Chinese remedy is evolving into many modern day uses and cures."

Persona

You also need to decide just how to present yourself as a writer to those who will read your work. Do you want to sound objective and fair, heated and passionate, sincere and persuasive, or informative and rational? The term persona is used to describe the identity that the speaker or writer adopts. As you know, we all play many roles, depending on the situations in which we find ourselves: with our parents, we may be quiet and reserved; with our peers, outgoing and comical, and so on. Similarly, you can be flexible about how you portray yourself in your writing, changing your persona with your purpose and audience. First, establish your credibility by being careful and thorough in your research and by showing that you have done your homework and understand what you are writing about. Then, prepare your finished product with care and attention to detail. If you do not, your readers will assume that you are sloppy and careless and will largely discount anything you have to say. Many job applicants never even make it to the interview stage because their letters of application convey the subliminal message "here is a person who is careless and inconsiderate of others."

After discussions with her classmates and teacher, Kauleen decided that she wished to adopt a persona that reflected her balanced and fair appraisal of the medical treatment known as acupuncture. She felt that the public held many negative stereotypes and preconceptions about the use of acupuncture that she wanted to dispel by sounding logical and straightforward in her presentation of the facts.

Audience

Identifying those who may be reading your writing will help you to make decisions about what to include or not include in your research paper. Those who are the most likely to read your writing make up your audience. For example, a social scientist writing for a professional journal may assume a readership made up of specialists. But if the social scientist, perhaps a demographer, is writing a report that will be read by the vice president of an marketing firm, for example, the social scientist may not be able to assume that his or her reader is a subject expert; thus, he or she must take care to define terms and to write clearly for the nonspecialist audience.

In the case of a college research paper, the instructor of the course may suggest an appropriate audience or may in fact be the primary audience. You will wish to discuss the paper's potential audience with your teacher. If the instructor is the intended audience, you should assume that the instructor is knowledgeable about the subject, reasonably intelligent, and particularly interested in the accuracy of the research.

Take time before writing to consider carefully who will read your research paper. Your readers make a difference to you, both in how you approach your topic (Are my readers novices or experts in the field?) and in the tone you adopt (Are my readers likely to agree with me or must I win them over to my point of view?). If your instructor has made no stipulations about the intended audience for your research paper, you should discuss the issue of audience with him or her. If your teacher is the target audience, it is especially important for you to know whether or not your teacher will be reading as a nonexpert (a novice in the field) or will assume the role of a knowledgeable expert. Your decisions about what to include in the paper and what level of tone and diction to adopt will depend on whether you are writing for an expert or novice audience.

Subject Matter

The most important component of the rhetorical situation, however, is the subject matter. Although no piece of writing exists in isolation (hence the need for analyzing the purpose, persona, and audience), the content that you are presenting to your audience will be the core of any piece you are writing. You must decide from the mass of material you discover in your research what to include in your written presentation. These decisions are based on your starting question, your analysis and evaluation of your sources, and your thesis statement. Knowing what your ultimate goal is, how you wish to sound, and who your readers are will help you decide what source materials to use.

Appropriate Language or Tone

Knowing your purpose, persona, audience, and subject matter will lead you also into appropriate decisions about language and tone.

If your purpose is to inform a general audience on a technical subject, you will need to take particular care with defining terms and using general words in place of technical jargon. You might also consider providing your readers with a glossary of terms to help them through technical information.

If you are addressing an audience of specialists, your rhetorical decisions about language and tone will be quite different. In this case you may wish to use technical vocabulary to identify yourself with the expert audience and to build your own credibility. You will need to take care not to bore an expert reader by providing too much background information, which such readers will not need.

ORGANIZATION

Once you have gathered and evaluated source materials on your topic, completed your preliminary writing assignments, and analyzed the rhetorical situation, you can begin to organize your ideas. During the planning stages, you need to decide how you will give pattern and order to your research paper. The importance of planning cannot be overemphasized. Readers will use your skeletal plan, which should appear in some form in the written research paper, to reconstruct your meaning. Many recent investigations into the reading process have shown that readers reconstruct meaning in writing by using organizational plans, that is, explicit directional signals left by the writer in his or her work.

There is no one right way to make order out of the mass of material you have gathered in your research. Some people find that just beginning to write helps them to "discover" a direction and a pattern. Others prefer to outline and to organize or sort their notes by categories. Some writers spread their notes in seemingly random piles across the desktop; others sort notecards neatly by topics. Eventually, regardless of the process, you want to be able to write a thesis statement that captures succinctly the main point you wish to make in your paper.

REVISING YOUR RESEARCH PAPER

Important work still remains on your paper once you have completed a rough draft. You must revise the paper to make the most effective possible presentation of the research. Your readers expect you to be clear and correct in your presentation so that they are not distracted by confusing language or incorrect punctuation. Read your rough draft several times, both on the computer screen and on hard copy. Each time you read it, pay attention to a different aspect of the paper for possible revision and correction. At first, when reading your rough draft pay attention to the overall structure and style of the paper; the second time through, check grammar and punctuation; the third time, make sure source materials (paraphrases and quotes from sources) are incorporated smoothly and accurately into the text. Finally, consider formal details such as conventions of documentation, format, and presentation. After your paper has been typed and spell-checked, proofread it several times to catch and correct all typographical or transcription errors.

Revising for Structure and Style

The first time you read your draft, pay attention to the organizational structure and overall content of the paper. At this point, decide whether you need to make any major changes in the order of the ideas or whether you should alter the tone. Use the power of your word processing program, in particular its cut and paste functions, to accomplish quickly and easily these global changes. A helpful acronym to keep in mind as you revise for such large issues is EARS: *E*liminate, *A*dd, *R*earrange, and *S*ubstitute.

Do not be afraid to eliminate irrelevant material from your paper. Your teacher will prefer a paper that is tightly focused to one padded with irrelevant details. Conversely, if you discover a section of your paper that seems thin, do not hesitate to add more information: more evidence to support an idea, more explanation to clarify an idea, and so on. Be sure that the major sections of the paper are arranged in a logical order. If there seems to be any confusion, rearrange major sections. Finally, if you find an example or a piece of evidence that does not seem persuasive in the context of the paper, substitute a new example for the one you currently have.

Remember, your rough draft is exactly that—rough. It is important for you to read it critically now so that you can improve the overall presentation of your ideas. Share your draft with a friend, spouse, teacher, classmate, or coworker. Another reader can provide insights to your paper that may be very helpful to you as your revise. The following list of questions can guide both you and others as they read your draft:

1. Is my title descriptive and does it relate to the paper?
2. Is my introduction complete? Does it make the reader want to read on?
3. Is my thesis clearly stated early in the paper so that the reader knows what to expect?
4. Is the organizational pattern of the paper clearly marked for the reader by subheadings or directional signals?

5. Are the various sections of the paper linked by good transitional words and phrases?
6. Have I used a variety of evidence as appropriate: examples, analyses, primary or secondary data, analogies, illustrations, narratives, descriptions?
7. Do the sections of the paper appear in a logical order or do I need to rearrange the parts? Does the logic of the argument seem clear?
8. Is each section of the paper supported with sufficient data and evidence from the sources and from my primary research? Are sources integrated smoothly into the flow of the paper? Can the reader tell where sources stop and my own writing begins?
9. Is my conclusion adequate? Does it return to the thesis and highlight the answer to the starting question that motivated the research?
10. Have I demonstrated a depth of analysis and complexity of thought concerning the topic such that readers will feel significantly taught by me?

Rework any troublesome aspects of the paper. If a particular section of the paper lacks sufficient evidence, go back to the library for some appropriate supporting material. If you are unsure about the tone of your paper, the clarity of the language, or the presentation of your ideas, ask for specific advice from other readers. Such outside readings of your work can sometimes provide the distance needed for an objective evaluation.

You may wish to try the technique of reverse outlining as a way of seeing any global structural problems in your draft. To reverse outline, number each paragraph in your draft. Then summarize in one sentence the essential content of each paragraph. In this way you may discover sections out of sequence or paragraphs on the same topic many pages apart. Or, if you are having difficulty summarizing a particular paragraph, you may find you have tried to cover too much information and need to divide a longer paragraph into a series of shorter, more focused paragraphs.

Improving Paragraphs

As previously suggested, you first look at the overall structure and content of your paper. Then begin to narrow the scope of your revising to individual paragraphs. Check to be sure that each paragraph has a single major focus and that the ideas within the paragraph are all related to that focus. Focusing your paragraphs in this way is a great aid to your reader. When this is done, a new paragraph indicates a change to a new idea or change in direction. Often, the first sentence of each paragraph serves as a transitional sentence, bridging the gap between the ideas in the two separate paragraphs. This is the time to check for transitions between paragraphs as well as paragraph focus. As you revise your paragraphs, ask yourself the following questions:

1. Does each paragraph relate to the overall point of my paper?
2. Does each new paragraph contain its own internal focus or coherence?
3. Does the first sentence of each paragraph offer a bridge or transition from the previous paragraph?
4. Is the language used in each paragraph concrete and clear? Are there unnecessary words or phrases that I should delete?
5. Is the tone of each paragraph objective? Do I sound interested and concerned about the subject but not overly emotional?

Improving Sentences

In continuing to narrow the scope of your revising, look at individual sentences within your paper. Revise any sentences that seem awkward or confusing. In general, the more simply and directly you state your ideas, the better. Do not use overly complex sentence structures—they will only confuse your reader. Any very long sentences may need to be broken down into shorter sentences. On the other hand, a series of short, choppy sentences may be more effective if rewritten as a single long sentence. Reading your draft aloud—to yourself or to someone else—can often help you to "hear" problematic sentences. Or perhaps your teacher can make additional suggestions about revising your sentence style.

Improving Words

Careful attention to wording in your paper will help you to most accurately report your research findings or review the literature for your readers. Look at individual words in your paper with an eye toward spotting confusing vocabulary or unnecessary jargon. If you are writing to a nonspecialist readership, take care to define any terms that might be unfamiliar to a general reader and replace any jargon specific to a field or discipline with more common words. As a general rule of thumb in social science writing, be simple and be concise. If you can write your findings in simple and direct language, it is a sure sign that you have come to grips with your subject and understand it thoroughly yourself. Often language that seems obscure reflects an underlying muddiness in the writer's thinking.

Verbs

A conventional usage for verb tenses has grown up over the years in social science writing. When reporting your own findings, use the *past* tense; when reviewing the published work of others, use the *present* tense:

I *observed* the subjects for twenty-four hours.

Sturkie (1986) *shows* that radioactive carbon *is lost* from organic materials at a predictable rate.

In much social science writing the intended clarity of expression may be lost behind empty verbs and passive constructions. Verbs are one part of speech that often cause writers problems. Performing these few simple editing tasks with the verbs in your research paper will vastly improve your own writing.

Content Verbs versus Empty Verbs

The verb "to be" (is, was, were, am, are) asserts a state of being, telling us only that something exists. Because the "to be" verb in its various forms essentially has become empty of meaning, you should attempt to replace "to be" verbs with content verbs that do convey meaning.

EXAMPLES:

Original—with empty "be" verb

It is the custom for visitors to remove their shoes before entering a Japanese home.

Revision—with content verb

Visitors customarily remove their shoes before entering a Japanese home.

Original—with empty "be" verb

Many planes are twenty years old and will have passed their life expectancy of ten to fourteen years.

Revision—with content verb

Now twenty years old, many planes have long since passed their life expectancy of ten to fourteen years.

Action Verbs versus Nominalizations

Many social science writers slow down their readers by using complex nouns in their sentences instead of the more active verbs that those nouns come from. For example, *decision* is the noun form (nominalization) of the verb *to decide,* and *invasion* is the noun form of *to invade.* Somehow writers have gotten the erroneous impression that the use of nominalizations makes their writing sound more important or official. Changing your verbs into nouns, however, robs them of their power and motion, thus slowing down the reader's progress. Whenever possible, change nominalizations to action verbs.

EXAMPLES:

Original—Sentence with nominalization
This land has the appearance of being arid.

Revision—Sentence with action verb
This land appears arid.

Original—Sentence with nominalization
He finally came to his decision. He would run for office.

Revision—Sentence with action verb
He finally decided to run for office.

Active Voice versus Passive Voice

The passive voice can be used effectively in writing when we either do not know who the subject is or don't want the subject known, as in the following:

Passive: The measurement of fat content *was used* to determine the energy content of the body. [by whom?]

Active: *We measured* fat content in the body to determine the energy content.

Passive: The fusing of the cusps *is often accompanied by* calcium deposits that further restrict the flow through the valve.

Active: Calcium deposits that further restrict the flow through the valve often *accompany* the fusing of the cusps.

Although passive voice has a legitimate function, it is often overworked in writing. To keep the pace of your writing moving along and to provide your readers with often essential information, try to use the active voice whenever possible.

Commonly Misused Words

The following words are frequently misused in social science writing.

A/An: Indefinite article, used to introduce a noun. *A* appears before a noun beginning with a consonant: a fish, a hypothesis, a poem; *An* appears before a noun beginning with a vowel or un-pronounced *h*: an hour, an apple, an order

Due to: Correctly used following a subject to attribute something to that subject.

Correct usage: The infant's decreased weight is *due to* its lack of food.

Incorrect usage: *Due to* its lack of food, the infant decreased in weight.

Compare:

1. Followed by *to* when comparing two similar people or things or implying an analogy.

    Correct usage: He *compared* the Hatfields *to* the McCoys.

2. Followed by *with* when comparing details of very similar or very dissimilar people or things.

    Correct usage: When compared *with* the McCoys, the Hatfields are more efficient farmers.

Data: Data is the plural form; *datum* is the singular.

Different from: preferred usage (*different than* is the less-preferred option)

Effect/Affect: Effect is the noun form, meaning results: The *effects* of too little sleep . . . Affect is the verb form, meaning influence: The play *affected* us deeply.

Index: Index is the singular form; the plural form is *indexes* as in book indexes, or *indices* as in measurable quantities.

Over/Under: not to replace *more* or *less than* when describing quantities.

Correct usage: We found *more than* 60% deviation from the norm.

Incorrect usage: We found *over* 60% deviation from the norm.

Parameter: Has a special meaning in mathematics and statistics; do not use loosely for variable, quantity, quality, determinant, or feature.

Percent: May be a noun, adjective, or adverb. When used with numbers, use the symbol. Correct: 98%. Incorrect: 98 percent.

Percentage: Noun, meaning part of the whole as expressed in hundredths, as in the *percentage* of red blood cells.

Correct usage: *percent* error (adjective)

Incorrect usage: *percentage* error

Significant/Significance: In social science papers, confine the use of this term to statistical judgment; do not use loosely for important, notable, or distinctive.

Editing for Grammar, Punctuation, and Spelling

Once you have revised the overall structure and style of your paper, you are ready to read the paper again, this time with an eye to grammar, punctuation, and spelling. It is important to present your ideas clearly, but it is equally important to present your ideas correctly. A reader will discount you as either ignorant or careless if your work is full of grammatical errors.

As you read your paper again, ask yourself the following questions:

1. Is the grammar of each sentence correct? Does each sentence contain subjects and predicates?
2. Do subjects and verbs agree?
3. Are pronouns clear and unambiguous in their reference?
4. Is the overall punctuation correct?
5. Have I punctuated and cited quotes and paraphrases correctly?
6. Are there any words that I need to look up in the dictionary, either for meaning or for spelling?
7. Have I used the active rather than the passive voice? Are my verbs vivid action words rather than empty "to be" verbs or nominals?
8. Have I varied sentence style and avoided repetition?
9. Does each sentence flow smoothly without being awkward, wordy, or confusing?
10. Is the format of my paper correct, including the title page, body of the text, endnotes, or bibliography page?

Mechanical Errors

It would be helpful for you to refer to a recent grammar and usage handbook for questions of English grammar, punctuation, and syntax. Use a dictionary to check the meaning of individual words and run spell-check with each draft. Take the time now to look carefully for all problems in your writing. As always, errors in grammar, punctuation, syntax, and spelling detract from your message and make a negative impression on your reader. A paper full of grammatical or spelling errors signals to the reader that the authority of the writer, and hence the authority of the research, is questionable. Listed below are a few of the most commonly made mechanical errors in social science writing:

1. Punctuation

   Commas

   a. Use a comma to separate long introductory material in a sentence from the rest of the sentence:

      Because of increased serum cholesterol levels, arteries within the circulatory system may form fatty lesions.

   b. Use commas to set off interrupting material from the rest of the sentence:

      This deposit of plaque, and the cellular proliferation of smooth muscle, can become a large bulge in the artery.

   c. Use commas to separate items in a series:

      Serum cholesterol measures may predict the risk for infarction, death from coronary heart disease, and all-cause mortality.

   d. Use a comma to separate independent clauses joined by a conjunction (and, but, or, for, nor, yet):

      This risk is more apparent in cardiac patients, but it is also apparent in healthy subjects.

      DO NOT use a comma to separate two independent clauses WITHOUT a conjunction:

      Incorrect: This risk is more apparent in cardiac patients, it is also apparent in healthy subjects.

   Dashes (typewritten as two hyphens --) The dash is used to set off nonessential elements in a sentence. It is more emphatic than either commas or parentheses:

      I welcome your reactions to the candidates—either orally or in writing—at any time following their campus visit.

   Semicolons are used in the following three cases:

   a. To join two independent clauses:

      This risk is more apparent in cardiac patients; it is also apparent in healthy subjects.

   b. To connect two independent clauses joined with a conjunctive adverb (however, nevertheless, moreover, furthermore):

      The benefits of high density lipoproteins is well documented; however, some have questioned the effects of very low levels of cholesterol.

c. As a "super-comma" in a series already containing commas:

The patients were given low-fat diets of complex carbohydrates; lean meats, fish, and poultry; and fat-free dairy products.

Colons are used mainly to introduce items in a series:

Their diet consisted of the following items: lean meats, fish, poultry, and grains.

The colon may also be used to introduce a direct quote:

In the Framingham study, the following is stated: "A relationship between cholesterol levels and prognosis in men and women does exist" (Jones 1992, p. 55).

2. Italics (or underline)

a. Use italics to indicate foreign words and phrases:

ad nauseum, in vitro, et alium

b. Use italics to indicate a word or phrase you wish to emphasize:

The depth at which a subject is placed into the chamber *can* alter your results.

3. Abbreviations

Typically, in social science writing terms of measurement in the text are abbreviated if they are preceded by a number. The same symbol is used for either singular or plural and no period is used:

1 hr (one hour)

12 hr (twelve hours)

3 l (3 litres); m = meter, min = minute, s = second, wk = week, year = yr, month = mo, day = da or d.

Do not abbreviate the name of a unit of measure that follows a spelled-out number, as at the start of a sentence:

Ten litres were required for proper dosing.

4. Parentheses

a. Use parentheses to refer to information in a table of figure in the text: (see Figure 1) or (Table 2).

b. Use parentheses to enclose a comment or explanation that is structurally independent of the rest of the sentence:

Roby (1989) also used total body immersion on the subjects in his study.

c. Use parentheses to label enumerations within a paragraph:

(1) (2)

    d. Use parentheses for internal citations:

        Fat content varies with age, sex, and nutrition (Sturkie, 1986).

  5. Brackets

      Use brackets to enclose information within parentheses:

        Hostility in the group toward one student was palpable (twice as may criticisms [Schmidt-Nielsen, 1990]).

  6. Numbers

    a. A decimal number of less than one should be written with a zero (0) preceding the decimal point:

        Thirty subjects had a narrow range of weight and their probability was lower, 0.676.

    b. Spell out a number that occurs at the beginning of a sentence:

        Fifteen of the subjects were weighed with their clothing still on.

    c. Numbers that modify an adjective should be written as a whole number and separated from the adjective with a hyphen:

        The weight of the males was monitored for a 5-year period.

    d. Numerical values are customarily identified by the letter n (or N):

        The subjects (n = 15) were interviewed in a neutral setting.

    e. Day of the month typically precedes the month. No commas are used:

        We monitored the males from 10 July 1994 to 10 January 1995.

In most situations use words for numbers one through nine and numerals for larger numbers. Treat ordinal numbeqrs as you would cardinal numbers: third, fourth, 33rd, 54th.

REWRITING YOUR PAPER
USING WORD PROCESSING

Using a computer word processing program to revise your research paper has many advantages. Using word processing, you can quickly and easily create a paper that is as attractive and free of distracting errors as possible. Some writers compose their research papers directly at the computer, perhaps using the research database they have already created in their computer research notebooks. Others type a rough draft into the computer for revising. Using word processing makes changing your paper easier, since it allows you to eliminate, add, rearrange, and substitute material, altering individual words, sentences, paragraphs, and even whole sections of the paper without having to recopy or retype.

Revising with Word Processing

Word processing allows you to move material in your paper from one location to another. Before doing so, however, be sure you have made a backup copy of your file so that you don't inadvertently lose part of your text. Once you have moved the material (typically using the cut and paste functions), be sure to read the revised version very carefully and make any changes needed to smoothly integrate the new material into the existing text. When revising for structure and style or to improve paragraphs, sentences, and words, you will find your word processing program's text manipulation features your greatest assets.

Editing with Word Processing

Word processing also makes editing for grammar, punctuation, and spelling easier. Most word processing programs now offer their users a spell-check feature, which is extremely helpful in identifying typographical errors. You should get in the habit of running spell-check several times as you are drafting your paper. Remember, though, that the spell-check feature does not identify words that you have inadvertently misused, such as homonyms: *there* for *their*, or *its* for *it's*, and so on. You still need to proofread very carefully yourself, even after using spell-check.

Another helpful tool for editing is your word processor's thesaurus. If you find you are overusing a particular word, you can use the thesaurus to supply alternatives. Or perhaps you find the verbs you have used are not as vivid and active as they could be; the thesaurus can suggest other verbs with similar meanings. Again, a note of caution: don't use a word suggested by a thesaurus that you don't know, because it might have connotations or slight variations in meaning that do not make sense in the particular context of your writing.

Grammar-Checking Software

Special software programs are now available that can help you edit and proofread your paper for selected stylistic or grammatical problems. For example, *Grammatik* and other similar programs will identify excessive use of inactive "to be" verbs, overuse of prepositions, vague words or jargon, and so on. However, the so-called grammar-checking programs currently available can be misleading to writers.

The kinds of writing problems that such programs can check are very limited. For example, they are virtually useless at checking punctuation because they are not sophisticated enough to really analyze the underlying grammar of each sentence. Only you, the writer, can do that. So, if you use a grammar-check feature, be aware of what it can and cannot do.

Bibliography and Footnote Software

Many word processing programs currently on the market offer features to help you generate the footnotes, endnotes, or bibliography for your paper. I have found these features only marginally useful in my own writing, but I know some writers use them quite extensively. If you are using footnotes, having the word processing program automatically place them at the bottom of the appropriate page can be a big help. However, the documentation software is only as good as the information you give it, that is, you still need to type in to the computer all of the bibliographical information. The software then manipulates the information, placing it in the proper order and formatting it appropriately. You need to be aware that the documentation style built into the software may not be the same style as you need to use for your discipline. Again, you should be the final judge of what is the correct documentation format for your paper.

If you have access to computer word processing, you may want to investigate some of the software previously discussed that is designed to help you with your writing. But do not take a computer program's advice as gospel; you cannot count on a computer to know what is best for your own writing; only you can know that.

Incorporating Reference Materials

The earlier section on writing the rough draft suggested that you not worry about the smooth incorporation of quoted material until you began revising your paper. We have now reached the stage at which you should double-check all of the source material in your paper to be sure you have incorporated it smoothly and appropriately into the flow of your ideas. Your source material should be primarily in the form of paraphrases and summaries that you use to reinforce your own points. Even though they are written in your own words, both paraphrases and summaries still require documentation (identification of the source either through in-text citations or footnotes or endnotes). Putting source material into your own words greatly improves the flow of your paper, because the paraphrase style will blend with your own writing style and thus be consistent throughout.

You should use direct quotation very sparingly. Reading strings of direct quotations is extremely distracting; using excessive quotation creates a choppy, disjointed style. Furthermore, it leaves the impression that you as a writer know nothing and are relying totally on what others have said on your topic. The better alternative is to incorporate paraphrases and summaries of source material into your own ideas both grammatically and logically. At this time, check your paper to be sure you have documented all source material accurately and fairly. By following the documentation style outlined in Chapter 6, you will be able to produce a paper that is correctly and accurately documented for your chosen academic discipline. In general, remember to document both completely and consistently, staying with one particular documentation style.

Incorporating Direct Quotes

At times you may want to use direct quotes in addition to paraphrases and summaries. To incorporate direct quotes smoothly, observe the following general principles. However, it would be wise to also consult the style manual of your discipline for any minor variations in quotation style.

1. When your quotations are four lines in length or less, surround them with quotation marks and incorporate them into your text. When your quotations are longer than four lines, set them off from the rest of the text by indenting five spaces from the left and right margins and triple-spacing above and below them. You do not need to use quotation marks with such block quotes. (Note: In some disciplines, block quotes are customarily indented ten spaces from the left margin only and double-spaced throughout.) Follow the block quote with the punctuation found in the source. Then skip two spaces before the parenthetical citation. Do not include a period after the parentheses.
2. Introduce quotes using a verb tense that is consistent with the tense of the quote. (A woman of twenty admitted, "I really could not see how thin I was.")
3. Change a capital letter to a lower-case letter (or vice versa) within the quote if necessary. (She pours her time and attention into her children, whining at them to "eat more, drink more, sleep more.")
4. Use brackets for explanations or interpretations not in the original quote. ("Evidence reveals that boys are higher on conduct disorder [behavior directed toward the environment] than girls.")
5. Use ellipses (three spaced dots) to indicate that material has been omitted from the quote. It is not necessary to use ellipses for ma-

terial omitted before the quote begins. ("Fifteen to twenty percent of anorexia victims die of direct starvation or related illnesses . . . [which] their weak, immuneless bodies cannot combat.")

6. Punctuate a direct quote as the original was punctuated. However, change the end punctuation to fit the context. (For example, a quotation that ends with a period may require a comma instead of the period when it is integrated into your own sentence.)

7. A period, or a comma if the sentence continues after the quote, goes inside the quotation marks. (Although Cathy tries to disguise "her innate evil nature, it reveals itself at the slightest loss of control, as when she has a little alcohol.") When the quote is followed with a parenthetical citation, omit the punctuation before the quotation mark and follow the parentheses with a period or comma: Cal has "recognized the evil in himself, [and] is ready to act for good" (Cooperman 88).

8. If an ellipsis occurs at the end of the quoted material, add a period before the dots. (Cathy is "more than Woman, who not only succumbs to the Serpent, but becomes the serpent itself . . . as she triumphs over her victims. . . .")

9. Place question marks and exclamation points outside the quotation marks if the entire sentence is a question or an exclamation. (Has Sara read the article "Alienation in *East of Eden*"?)

10. Place question marks and exclamation points inside the quotation marks if only the quote itself is a question or exclamation. (Mary attended the lecture entitled "Is Cathy Really Eve?")

11. Use a colon to introduce a quote if the introductory material prior to the quote is long or if the quote itself is more than a sentence or two long.

```
Steinbeck puts it this way:

[long quote indented from margin]
```

12. Use a comma to introduce a short quote. (Steinbeck explains, "If Cathy were simply a monster, that would not bring her in the story.")

Formatting and Printing Using Computers

Besides helping you as a writer, word processing can also help you create a text that is professional in appearance. However, attention to format should be the last consideration of your writing process. Too often, writers using word processing spend excessive amounts of their time playing with the appearance of the text, varying the fonts, for example, rather than concentrating on content. Of course, in the end you must attend to both form and content if you want to communicate effectively with your readers.

Many word processing programs offer formatting features such as underlining, boldface, italics, and so on, with which you can vary the appearance of your text and highlight important information. Be certain, however, that you check with your instructor to ascertain his or her preferences for format style before varying the style too much. Your main goal should be to make your paper professional in appearance. Thus, an English Gothic typeface that prints in scrolling capital letters, for example, would not be appropriate for a research paper. Nor are margins that are justified (even) on the right of the page typically appropriate for a formal paper. It is best to be conservative and justify left margins only.

Proofreading

Once your paper has been typed to your teacher's specifications and you have run your word processing program's spell-check feature, you will still need to proofread carefully for any errors not caught by the computer. For example, spell-check cannot tell you if you have used "their" when you should have used "there." It is best to print out a clean copy of your paper after making all of your proofreading corrections. However, your teacher may not object to your making a few minor corrections on the paper, preferring that you correct any errors, even though this may necessitate some handwriting on the typed page, rather than leaving them uncorrected.

One helpful way to proofread for typing errors is to begin at the bottom of the page and read up one line at a time. In this way, you keep yourself from reading for meaning and look only at the form of the words. You can spot errors more easily when you are not actually reading the paper. If you are proofreading on a computer screen, you can use your search command to search for periods from the bottom of the text upwards. In this way, your computer's cursor will skip to the previous sentence, thus reminding you to read it independently.

Keep your dictionary handy and refer to it whenever you have any doubt about the appropriate use of a word. Use your grammar and usage handbook to double-check any last minute questions about grammar and punctuation. If you have access to grammar-check software, such as *Writer's Helper, Correct Grammar,* or *Grammatik,* it is sometimes helpful to run it on your paper, keeping in mind the cautions about such programs that were discussed previously.

It is impossible to overstress the importance of careful proofreading by you. Even if the paper was word processed or typed by a professional typist, you will probably find errors when proofreading. Since you are the paper's author, any errors are your responsibility, not the computer's or the typist's. It is a good idea to save early drafts of your paper even after the paper has been typed. Early drafts serve as a record of your thinking and your work on the paper. If you have taken care at every stage of the revision process, your paper will be one you can be justifiably proud of.

CONSIDERING FORMAL DETAILS

The formal details outlined in the paragraphs that follow incorporate some general principles in research writing. However, it would be wise to also consult the relevant style manual for your field to discover any minor variations from this format. The model papers in Chapters 4 and 6 adhere to the formal conventions of their respective disciplines, so you may also use these as a resource.

Always type research papers or have them typed for you. Use a standard typeface or font and a fresh printer ribbon. It might be wise to ascertain whether or not your teacher prefers that papers not be printed on dot matrix printers. Sometimes these are light and difficult to read. If possible, print your final copy on a laser printer for a professional appearance and ease of reading. The paper should be a standard weight and size (8½ × 11 inches). If you do not have a self-correcting typewriter or a word processor, use Liquid Paper or correction tape to correct errors.

Spacing

Use only one side of the paper and double space all the way through, even for long quotes that are indented in the text [Note: Styles vary]. Leave four blank lines between major sections, between heading and section, and above and below indented, long quotes (more than four lines of text). Also, double space the endnote page (if used) and references page. Some journals ask writers to submit their papers with each section beginning on a separate sheet of paper (e.g., Abstract, Introduction). This is usually not necessary for a student paper, but do put any figures or tables on separate pages, numbered consecutively (one set of numbers for figures; another for tables). Place these illustration pages after the Works Cited page for reference.

Margins

Use a margin 1 to 1.5 inches wide on all sides of each sheet. Your word processing program allows you to set the margins appropriately. If you are typing your paper, use a typing guide (a sheet of paper that goes behind the sheet you are typing on and whose dark ruled lines show through), set the margins on your typewriter, or mark each sheet with a pencil dot one inch from the bottom so you will know when to stop typing on a page. Sophisticated word processing programs will help you format the pages appropriately. In particular, if you are using footnotes, these can be generated automatically by some word processing programs, which will leave the appropriate amount of space for footnotes on each page. If you are typing footnotes at the bottom of the page yourself, plan your bottom margins very carefully to allow room for the notes. Generally, endnotes are easier to type and perfectly acceptable in most cases.

Title

Ask your instructor whether you need a title page. If the answer is yes, find out what information should appear there. Generally, title pages contain three kinds of identifying information: the title of the paper, author identification, and course identification (including date). If you do not need a separate title page, put your name, date, assignment name, and any other identifying information on the upper right-hand corner of the first page. Center the title on the first page three or four lines below the identifying information or, if you use a separate title page, one inch from the top of the page. The title should not be underlined, surrounded by quotation marks, or typed in capital letters. Leave three or four lines between your title and the beginning of the text. Some instructors will require you to type an outline or Table of Contents immediately after your title. Check to see if your instructors would like such an outline included.

Numbering

Number each page starting with the first page of text after the title page. (Note: some styles omit the page number from page 1.) Place the numbers in the upper right-hand corners or centered at the bottom of the pages. Your word processing program allows you to automatically number your pages and to suppress numbering on any pages where they are not needed. For example, you typically don't need to number the endnote page and the references page. Rather, identify them with the appropriate heading centered one inch from the top of the page and followed by three or four blank lines. Some styles recommend headers along with the page numbers (for example, Hult - 2). Check your word processing manual for help in generating such automatic headers.

Indentation

Use uniform indentation for all paragraphs (five spaces is standard). Indent long quotes (more than four lines long) five spaces from both right and left margins or ten spaces from the left margin only. Indent the second and subsequent lines of the reference-list entries five spaces. Leave two spaces between each sentence and after a colon or semicolon. Divide words at the end of lines according to standard rules. Use your dictionary if you are unsure of where to divide a word.

The Abstract

An abstract is a very short summary of a paper, usually one tenth to one twentieth the length of the whole. The purpose of an abstract is to condense the paper into a few, succinct lines. Thus, the reader must be able to understand the essence of the paper from reading just the abstract, without actually reading the paper. Your abstract should cover the purpose of your paper as well as the major topics you discuss. To write an abstract, follow the same general procedure you used to write a summary paper. However, you will need to compress information into a few compact sentences. Even though the information in your abstract is necessarily densely packed, it should still be readable and understandable.

The Endnote Page

If your paper will have endnotes, type them on a separate page immediately after the text of your paper (and before the references page). Center the title, "Notes" or "Endnotes," one inch from the top of the page, and type it in capital and lower-case letters (not all capitals). Do not use quotation marks or underlining. Leave three or four blank lines between the title and the first line of your notes. Type the notes in consecutive order based on their appearance in the text. Indent the first line of the note five spaces from the left margin, type the superscript number, and leave a space before beginning the note. For any run-over lines of each note, return to the left margin.

The References Page

Center the title "References," "Works Cited," or "Bibliography" and type it one inch from the top of the page in capital and lower-case letters (not all capitals). Do not use quotation marks or underlining. Leave three or four blank lines between the title and the first line of your references. The references themselves should be typed, double spaced, and listed in alphabetical order by the author's last name (or the title, if the author is not known). The references page follows the last page of your paper or the endnote page (if included) and need not be numbered.

The Annotated Bibliography

In some cases it is helpful to provide your readers with more information about the sources you used in your research than is typically given in a bibliography. An annotated bibliography serves this purpose. To construct an annotated bibliography, you would first compile all of your references, alphabetize them, and format them according to the documentation style for your discipline. Then, following each bibliographical entry, you would state in a sentence or two the gist of the source you had read and its relevance to your paper. An annotated bibliography can help your readers to decide which of your sources they would like to read themselves. It should not be difficult for you to annotate (that is, provide brief glosses) for sources that you have used to write your paper.

The Appendix

Material that may not be appropriate to the body of your paper may be included in an appendix. You may use the appendix for collations of raw data, descriptions of primary research instruments, detailed instructions, and so on. The appendix is located after the bibliography or references page and is clearly labeled. If there is more than one appendix, label them Appendix A, Appendix B, and so on. When referring to the appendix in the paper itself, do so in parentheses: (For a detailed description of the questionnaire, see Appendix A.)

Using Graphics

Sometimes you will find that you need to illustrate your work using graphics. Types of graphics include tables (usually showing quantitative data), figures (charts, graphs, or technical drawings), or illustrations (including photographs). You first need to determine whether or not your readers would benefit from the inclusion of a graphic. Sometimes repeating information in another form, such as a graphic, will help readers to remember it. The following principles may help you decide:

> Use a graphic when words alone cannot describe a concept or object adequately.
>
> Use a graphic to summarize an important point.
>
> Use a graphic when it can help to conveniently display complex information.

You also should determine purposes for the graphic to accomplish and where it would best be included in your paper. To align your graphic, remember that the graphic should be easy to read and displayed with ample white space so that it stands out from the text background. You should refer at least once to each graphic, either directly or parenthetically, in the text itself. The graphic should be placed on the same page in which it is mentioned and labeled with both a title and a source. Number tables sequentially throughout your paper; if you are including both figures and tables, they should be numbered separately (e.g., Table 1, Table 2, Figure 1, Figure 2).

6

✦ ✦ ✦

Secondary Research Methods: Writing a Review Paper

As discussed in Chapter 1, the social sciences have as their goal the systematic study of human behavior and human societies. Social science researchers must have knowledge of current research being conducted by others in their field. That is why library work, using secondary sources, is also important. In the social science journals, researchers report their findings for scrutiny and replication by other researchers. As you become familiar with the tools used by social scientists to gain access to current research, several research principles and skills will be important to you. These skills include:

1. A familiarity with primary research techniques used by social scientists.
2. A familiarity with library research tools used by social scientists, including databases, bibliographies, and indexes.
3. The ability to synthesize and evaluate data and opinions from a variety of primary and secondary sources.
4. The ability to develop a thesis consistent with the evidence found in primary and secondary sources.
5. The ability to organize and write a paper that effectively presents and supports your thesis.
6. The ability to employ the formal conventions of research papers in the social sciences.

A GUIDE TO THE SOCIAL SCIENCE
RESEARCH PROCESS

Your first task is to choose a topic or research problem to investigate. If you are taking a social science course such as psychology or sociology, your textbook is a good place to start looking for research ideas. Remember that the inquiry process generally begins with a perceived incongruity, problem, or question. Perhaps something you read in your textbook or in a popular magazine such as *Psychology Today* will raise a question in your mind, or perhaps a particular issue will seem interesting or intriguing to you. In any case, you need to find a topic that will hold your interest and attention, a topic on which you are willing to spend considerable time and energy. Kirstin Roundy, whose research serves as the model for this chapter, became interested in the subject of DNA profiling when she read about it in a criminology class. Be sure you select a topic that will hold your interest and attention, preferably a topic that you already know something about, so that you will be an informed and objective reviewer.

Preparation

You need to gather the materials for your research, including a research notebook or index cards (if you plan to use them); then make a schedule that allows sufficient time for your research. Your interest in the topic will get you started, but you will still need to think about the problem you have posed for yourself and begin to propose ways to investigate it. For example, Kirstin began with the topic of DNA fingerprinting and its use in criminology. Kirstin, a frequent computer user, decided to develop a computer research notebook rather than take notes on index cards or in a notebook. She set up a database file on a computer disk to serve as the repository for information collected during the research. Her first entries in the research notebook file were her topic idea and starting research questions. Then she outlined for herself a search strategy, as described in this chapter.

Developing a Search Strategy

Kirstin had formulated some general questions about DNA profiling through reading for her class. She wanted to discover whether DNA profiling was foolproof and whether there were any regulations governing its application. Her library search began with a look at general background sources and moved to more specific works on DNA profiling. The following is an outline of Kirstin's search strategy (your particular search may differ somewhat from this outline):

Kirstin's Search Strategy

1. Look up DNA and genetics in background sources from the reference area of the library, including the *Henderson's Dictionary of Biological Terms*, 10th ed, and the *International Encyclopedia of Politics and Law*.
2. Look up reviews on the subject using *Current Contents: Life Sciences*.
3. Use the library online catalog to find books and documents on DNA profiling; be sure to check appropriate terminology in the Library of Congress Subject Headings.
4. Use databases and print indexes and abstracts for access to journal articles: the *Sociological Index*, the *Applied Science and Technology Index*. Search by subject headings from LCSH and by key words, such as DNA or forensic genetics.

✦ EXERCISE

Outline your own search strategy, beginning with general and working to specialized sources. You will also probably wish to proceed in reverse chronology, that is, beginning with the most recent sources and working your way back in time. Include any primary research (such as interviews or questionnaires) you might wish to use in your project. Draw up a research time schedule.

General Sources

Reading general information on your subject enables you to put it into context. It helps you focus your search and refine your starting questions. Reading specialized encyclopedias and dictionaries also helps you define what is considered common knowledge on your subject. Depending on your particular subject, you may be reading general encyclopedias, such as *Americana*, and specialized encyclopedias, such as *The Encyclopedia of Psychology*. Kirstin used the following background sources, which she listed in her computerized research notebook as the beginning of her working bibliography:

Henderson's Dictionary of Biological Terms, 10th
    ed. Eleanor Lawrence, ed. New York: John
    Wiley, 1989.

International Encyclopedia of Politics and Law.
    Archive Publishers. New York: State Mutual
    Book and Periodicals Services, 1987.

<u>Encyclopedia Americana</u>. International edition. New

York: Grolier, 1990.

At the end of each source, such as the encyclopedia mentioned above, you will usually find a list of bibliographic citations and references. This reference list can be an important place to locate key sources and reports written about your topic. List any promising references on your working bibliography, because later they may lead you to valuable information. It is not necessary for you to look up each entry on your working bibliography at this time.

Focusing Your Search

After you have read several general background sources about your subject, you are ready to narrow the subject of your review.

Kirstin, for example, decided to report on the current state of knowledge regarding DNA profiling in criminology. Kristin developed the following starting questions to guide her research: "Is DNA Profiling foolproof? What is involved in the process? Is it ethical? Are there any regulations that govern it?" These starting questions provided Kirstin with a direction for her research.

✦ EXERCISE

Define for yourself starting questions to guide your research. Use these questions as a place to begin—your research direction may change as you actually find and read your sources.

Since Kirstin's topic incorporated some elements of science as well as social science, she decided to use scientific reviews as a possible background source. A useful tool for finding current articles and reviews is the *Current Contents* journal, which indexes articles and reviews by discipline.

Current Contents publish weekly issues, which include the tables of contents from the latest journals in a particular discipline. The journals are indexed by key title words and by authors. In our library, the *Current Contents* journals are provided in a computerized database; they are also available in print. By typing "DNA" into the computer while searching the database for *Current Contents: Life Sciences*, Kirstin discovered the following recent articles, which she listed in her working bibliography:

Genetic identification, Jeffreys. <u>The Futurist</u>

22:51. May/June '88.

Genetics meets forensics, Ricki Lewis. <u>BioScience</u>
39:6-9 Jan '89.

The Library Catalog

At this point in your search you will want to use the library on-line catalog. First, use the catalog to help you track down the book sources you may have already listed on your working bibliography from background sources. Once in the database that lists your library's book holdings, you will indicate that you want the computer to search by title (for example, t = DNA technology in forensic science). If this book is available in your library, it will be listed, along with its call number to help you locate the book.

The most important and powerful use for the online catalog is its cross-referencing function: using the subject headings and key words to locate additional titles on the same or related topics. You want to instruct the computer to search for books on your subject (for example, s = DNA profiling) or by key word or combinations of key words (for example, k = DNA and forensics). [See also pp. 18–24 above.]

Kirstin used the LCSH (*Library of Congress Subject Headings*) list to discover headings under which her topic might be listed. She found the following headings to be useful: DNA, DNA fingerprints, and forensic genetics. Using these headings in the online catalog, Kirstin found the following titles:

Kirby, L. (1990) DNA <u>fingerprinting--An</u>

   <u>introduction</u>. New York: Stockton Press.

National Research Council. (1992). DNA technology

   in forensic science. Washington, D.C.: National

   Academy Press.

Office of Technology Assessment, Congress of the

   United States. (1990, July). Genetic witness:

   Forensic uses of DNA tests.

United States Senate. (1989, March). Genetic

   testing as a means of criminal investigation.

   Hearing before the subcommittee on the

   Constitution of the Committee on the Judiciary.

   One hundred first Congress, first session.

Available from: U.S. Government Printing Office.

Washington, D.C.: #J101-4.

Subject Indexes and Abstracts

Once you have gathered a substantial amount of information on your subject and noted several key references and authors, you are in a position to expand your working bibliography by gathering more-specialized information from magazine and journal articles. Providing access to such information is the principle function of the subject indexes.

The subject indexes, such as the *Social Sciences Index*, list articles published in a given year on a particular subject. These indexes may be available to you either online through a computer or in print.

Online Indexes and Abstracts

Most modern libraries rely heavily on databases to help patrons search for professional journal articles. Our library, for example, contains databases of all the indexes produced by the W. W. Wilson company; these databases can be searched by individuals via computer. Our screen initially shows a menu of databases: one for general periodicals; one for professional literature in the sciences, agriculture, and engineering; one for professional literature in the arts and humanities; and one for professional literature in the social sciences. After selecting the appropriate database for your topic, you can search the database using the subject headings you found while searching for books, or you can use key words and combinations of key words.

Other databases may be available in your library through computers that make use of compact disks (CD-ROMs). These databases usually index specialized professional articles. Our library, for example, currently offers patrons CD-ROM databases to search for articles in the areas of business, agriculture, education, medicine, psychology, natural resources, and wildlife. (Pages 30–31 provide a listing of indexes and abstracts that indicates which are likely to be available through computerized database searching.) Check with your library to find out whether any of these indexes via computer are available to you. Searching in this way is far more efficient and thorough than searching through print media.

Print Indexes

The subject indexes, such as *Social Sciences Index* or *Applied Science and Technology Index*, list articles published in a given year by subject and author. By using these indexes, you can search for citations to journal articles written on your topic. You should usually start with the most recent volume of the index and work your way back, looking up your topic in several volumes of the index.

The second type of print index you may need to use in your library search is the citation index. Through the use of the citation index, you can begin with a particular researcher's name and work your way forward to other researchers who have listed (cited) that researcher in their subsequent work. Citation indexes are relatively comprehensive listings of such citations. The key sources listed in other reference works are the cited sources in the citation index. Typically, you will know the names of key researchers on your topic after a thorough search of the encyclopedias and reviews of research. Then you can follow up by searching each volume of the citation index for citations to these key sources that have appeared since the original publication of the key source. In this fashion, you will quickly build your working bibliography. The important citation index for the social sciences is SSCI (*Social Sciences Citation Index*).

It may take you some time to become familiar with how the citation indexes work, but doing so will be well worth the effort. These indexes are a major tool in the social sciences. When using the citation index, you may find that the complete title of the citing source is omitted, so it may be difficult to know whether the article will turn out to be relevant to your search or not. By looking up the author's name in the source index for the same year, you may find a more complete listing. You should review each article later to determine its importance to your search.

A third important type of indexing service is abstracts. Kirstin found *Biological Abstracts* to be useful in her search. Abstracts go one step further than indexes by providing you with a short summary of the article, which can help you sort through your references for those that are the most appropriate for your own search. Some abstracts may be available on computers: *Psychology Abstracts,* for example, is available in a CD-ROM database called Pychlit. Check with your librarian to find out which abstracts in your library may be searchable via computer.

Primary Research

As a last step in your research, you may wish to conduct some primary research to reinforce the information gathered in your library search. (Primary research projects are discussed in detail in Chapter 4.) Some possible primary research projects might include interviews, observations, case studies, or questionnaires, depending on the nature of your research topic.

✦ EXERCISE

Conduct any primary research connected to your research project. Analyze your results and determine the best method of displaying them, whether in a graph, table, or discussion section in your paper.

Evaluation

It is important that you read and evaluate carefully each source located in your library search. (See Chapter 3, p. 54 for some evaluation suggestions.) It is not unusual for a book or article with a promising title to turn out to be something totally different from what you expected to find. You must continually sort through sources and discard any that are not relevant or useful to your search. If, after an initial screening, a book still looks useful, check it out at the circulation desk. In the case of articles, either photocopy them for later use or take notes from them in the library, since they generally are noncirculating materials and cannot be checked out. If your library does not carry a source you are interested in, ask the circulation librarian about the possibility of an interlibrary loan.

Taking Notes

As you begin to take notes on the sources, remember to record complete bibliographic information so that you will not need to look up a particular source again.

If you are taking notes in your research notebook, identify each source carefully. Put into quotation marks any information taken directly from the source and write down the exact page number on which the note was found at the end of the note itself. Also identify paraphrased or quoted material. Taking care at this stage is beneficial when you reach the actual writing stage of your research paper.

Illumination

Since you are actively seeking the answer to the starting question you posed at the beginning of your search, continually "talk to yourself" while researching. Try to understand and interpret the source information as you go, synthesizing data from numerous authors and sources, taking what is relevant and discarding what is not. This is where your research notebook can be of particular value to you. Take the time to write down your own thoughts and comments as you go; note for yourself those sources and ideas that you find particularly important or revealing. Think about your topic consciously but also allow yourself enough time to let your ideas brew in your subconscious mind. It is during this stage in your research that you are seeking the answer to your starting question. Gradually, you arrive at a tentative answer, a hypothesis or thesis that satisfactorily explains the question's answer as you see it. Or you may modify or completely change the hypothesis or thesis in light of what you ultimately find in your research.

This is the illumination stage of the inquiry process, wherein you begin to "see the light," that is, the answer to your question. Perhaps your answer is that there is no definitive answer, and that would be all right too. In such a case, you would provide the most likely hypotheses and argue the relative merits of each. At any rate, you would present your understanding of the subject in a thesis statement that explained the data you gathered. In your thesis, then, state your opinion, articulating what you believe based on the evidence you have gathered.

✦ EXERCISE

Write a thesis statement that articulates the tentative conclusion you have reached through your research. In your thesis, state your preliminary answer to the starting question posed at the beginning of your research. But, keep an open mind; you may find that as you actually begin drafting your paper, you may arrive at new insights.

Verification

Once you have defined a thesis statement for yourself, you will have a place to begin your actual written presentation of the research. As you write, however, you may find that the thesis statement needs to be revised in some way. The actual writing of the research paper may help you see things in new ways or discover meanings you had not thought of before you began writing. Actually writing down your ideas in a systematic fashion is an important way of verifying the research you have done. As you try to articulate in writing the understanding you have gained of your topic, you may find that there are gaps in your knowledge that you need to fill by further research, or you may find that the thesis you have articulated really does not seem to explain the research findings adequately. In either case, you need to go back to both your primary and secondary sources for further information and more thought. On the other hand, you may find that your writing has clarified your ideas, thereby verifying them both for you and your potential readers.

ORGANIZING AND WRITING THE
SOCIAL SCIENCE RESEARCH PAPER

A major task in writing a social science review is organizing the material you have gathered. It is your job to make sense of the information you found in your library search. Remember, you are trying to make the information accessible to your readers as well as objective and comprehensive. When Kirstin began to narrow her topic, she decided to focus on the reliability issue with DNA profiling. As she thought through the rhetorical situation, she decided that she wanted to convey to a lay audience not only how the DNA profiling process was discovered and implemented, but also the considerable controversy surrounding its current use in criminal cases.

After completing her library research, Kirstin articulated an answer to her starting question in the form of a thesis statement: "It is the purpose of this paper to further investigate the subject of DNA profiling; by discussing the DNA components and detailing the process involved with developing a genetic fingerprint, the reader will gain a general understanding of DNA profiling and the effects it has had on forensic science." This thesis statement provided Kirstin with an overall direction for her paper.

To understand the process of DNA profiling, Kirstin decided to first discuss the human genome and the origin of the DNA profiling process; then she would discuss the uses of the process as they have been developed in forensic science. This organizational plan made the information easily available to the reader. Kirstin divided each subsection with descriptive headings to further help the reader discern her organizational plan. Social science reviews often are subdivided in this way to allow the reader easy access to the information.

Organizing Your Materials

Once Kirstin had decided on the thesis statement and organizational plan, she grouped related information in her computerized research notebook, using the cut and paste functions of her word processor, under the headings she had decided on in planning her paper. Because all her information was stored in her computer research notebook, it was an easy matter to move blocks of material in the notebook using the block move (cut and paste) commands. (Be sure to make a backup file of your notebook before beginning to manipulate the information in this way.)

Kirstin moved to the end of the computer file any information that did not seem to fit into the paper, such as information she had gathered on the other uses of genetic fingerprinting besides those in criminal investigations. This material was not relevant to her particular thesis statement. To make a unified, coherent presentation of your research, you must discard any information that is irrelevant. With her preliminary plan set, Kirsten wrote a more detailed outline to guide her in writing the paper:

> Outline
> I. Introduction
> II. DNA fingerprinting
>   A. Background
>   1. DNA sample
>   a. how obtained?
>   b. what do geneticists do with it?
>   c. how can it be read?
>   d. what does it show?
>   B. Applications of information
>   1. Effects on criminals, police work
> III. Controversies of DNA fingerprinting
>   A. Need for standards
>   B. Violation of Privacy Act
> IV. Conclusion

Writing the First Draft

After you have completed your informal outline, you are ready to write the first draft of your research paper. Remember, your objective is to present to your readers the answer you have discovered to the starting question. Remind yourself at this time of the question that initially motivated your search. When writing your first draft, use concrete and simple language to explain your thesis and the supporting evidence you gathered in your research as objectively as you can. Your thesis statement and your outline will guide the writing of this first draft. You should remain flexible as you write and be open to any fresh insights you may have along the way.

As you are writing the first draft, it is important to make a note of which material comes from which sources. Do not be concerned at this point about the formal details of documentation; you can deal with that later. But do mark for yourself in the draft any ideas or words taken from your sources. Place any word or words you copy from a source in quotation marks, and after the quote write down the last name and the date of publication of the source and the page number of the quoted material (in parentheses). For example,

> "When performed properly, the technique is
> capable of providing strong evidence for solving
> crimes. We think it is a powerful tool for
> criminal investigations and for the exoneration
> of innocent individuals, and that it should
> continue to be used. . . ." (McKusick, as cited
> in Zurer, 1992b, p.4).

Similarly, document paraphrases and restatements of ideas taken from a source even though you have recast them in your own words:

> In a bulletin, "Crime in the United States
> 1987," the Federal Bureau of Investigations
> states that over 1.3 million violent crimes were
> reported in the United States during that year
> (Kirby, 1990, p.4).

For general information on planning, writing, and revising your social science research paper, refer to Chapter 5. Use the following information on documentation in the social sciences to make your citations. The model paper below illustrates the writing and documentation styles commonly used in the social sciences.

MANUSCRIPT PREPARATION (APA STYLE)

The *Publication Manual of the American Psychological Association* describes in great detail the types of articles typically written in the social sciences and the manuscript format of those articles. The major parts of a manuscript are the title page, abstract, introduction, body, references page, and appendix. I will briefly describe each section here, but please refer to the APA manual for a more detailed discussion. The sample paper beginning on p. 162 follows the APA style for manuscript preparation, so you may use it as a model for your own paper.

Title Page

Write a title that summarizes the main idea of the paper as simply (yet as completely) as you can. Do not use a clever or cute title, but rather, summarize the main idea of your paper in an informative title that could stand alone. Kirsten's title "Childhood Schizophrenia: A Family Problem" sums up quite well the main idea of her paper. You will also need to compress your title into a manuscript page header, usually the first two or three words of your title, that will serve to identify each page of your paper. Identify the title page with the manuscript page header and page number 1 in the upper right-hand corner of the page.

The title page should also present identifying information on the author (called the byline) and the course (when the paper is submitted as part of a course requirement). The title, author information, and course information should be centered on the page and evenly spaced. A running head should be listed at the top of the title page, flush left in all capital letters, one line below the manuscript page header and page number (see Kirsten's title page on p. 162).

Abstract

The second page of your paper will include an abstract that briefly summarizes the essential content (about 100 words long). The APA manual points out that an abstract should be accurate, self-contained, concise and specific, nonevaluative, coherent, and readable. By reading your abstract, the reader should get a clear sense of the information covered by your paper. The abstract is typed in a one-paragraph block on its own page with no paragraph indentations (see Kirsten's abstract on p. 163).

Text

Begin typing the text of your paper on a new page. Type the title, centered, in lower- and upper-case letters. Double space after the title. The text of your research paper begins on page 3 (which is listed along with the manuscript page header in the upper right-hand corner).

Introduction

The text of your paper should open with an introduction that makes a commitment to the reader about what is to come in the paper. A good introduction should lead the reader into the paper and usually concludes with your thesis statement. There is no need to label the introduction; just begin it immediately after your title.

Body

The body of your paper should flow logically and follow the organization set up by your outline. You may wish to divide your paper visually by using headings and subheadings. Such headings can help your reader to visually ascertain the importance of topics within your paper and their relationship to other topics covered. Your headings function much as an outline would, that is, they provide your reader with a sense of your paper's organizational structure.

The APA manual describes five levels of headings and subheadings. However, they suggest using just one or two levels for short papers such as your research paper. For one level of headings, center your headings in the middle of the page (double spaced above and below), using lower- and uppercase letters. For two levels of headings, use the centered headings (lower- and uppercase) for the main headings and use side headings (flush with the left margin), underlined, for the subheadings:

`Research Methods` *Main heading*

<u>`Procedures`</u> *Subheading*

See the sample student paper beginning on p. 162 for an example of using one level of headings.

References Page

The references page is a listing of all the articles and books you refer to in the body of your paper. Your reference to source information in your paper helps support your own ideas and conclusions by relating them to other authors' ideas and conclusions. Each author you cite in the text of your paper (in-text citations) must appear on your reference list; similarly, each reference on your list must be cited in your text at some point. That is, do not list any sources you used for background reading but did not cite in the paper itself. These sources will be listed on your working bibliography, however, so your teacher will know the extent and breadth of your reading on the topic.

The reference list begins on a new page. Type the word References in upper- and lower-case letters, centered at the top of the page. Double space the entire references page.

The APA format for references on the references page is provided in the section on Documentation in Social Science. If you have a source that is not modeled shown there, refer to the APA manual for the appropriate style.

Appendix

Sometimes additional information is included in an appendix to a paper. If you have conducted some primary research in connection with your project, the data you collected may be presented in an appendix, for example. However, you should include an appendix only if it will help your reader understand or evaluate something that you have discussed or presented in your paper.

DOCUMENTATION IN SOCIAL SCIENCE: THE AUTHOR/DATE STYLE (APA)

In the social sciences, the author/date method of documentation is standard. This format is outlined in *The Publication Manual of the American Psychological Association,* 4th ed., Washington, D.C.: American Psychological Association, 1994. The citations are included in the text and thus help the reader identify authorities and the dates of the research immediately. This form of documentation is particularly useful when you are citing books and articles but are not quoting or paraphrasing from them.

Internal Citation

At the appropriate place in the text, you will give the author's name, followed by a comma, a space, and the year of publication:

> Today, genetic fingerprinting has expanded
> into several aspects of the life sciences
> (Franklin-Barbajosa, 1992).

As an alternative that prevents monotony and improves readability, you can give the author's name in the text occasionally, supplying only the year in parentheses:

> As Thompson and Ford (1990) point out, DNA
> profiling is ready for the course.

When continuing to cite the same study within a paragraph, it is not necessary to keep repeating the date, as long as there are no other studies by authors with the same name with which it could be confused:

> In a study on DNA profiling, Thornton (1989)
> found . . . Thornton also describes

For paraphrases and direct quotations, follow the date with a page number:

> DNA profiling "is the greatest advance in
> crime-fighting technology since fingerprints"
> (Thompson and Ford, 1990, p. 38).

If your source has two authors, list the surnames of both authors:

> The field of forensics involves the
> application of given evidence to specific court
> cases (Thompson and Ford, 1990).

If your source has more than two authors, list all authors the first time a reference occurs; in subsequent citations, use the first author's name with "et al." (abbreviation for Latin et alii, "and others"):

First citation:

(Garfinkle, Garner, Schwartz, & Thompson, 1980)

Subsequent citation:

(Garfinkle et al., 1980)

If there is no author's name, use either the title or an abbreviated form of the title. Place the title in quotation marks. Use underline for the title of a periodical, book, brochure, or report:

> ("DNA Profiling," 1991)

If you have two articles with the same title, list the source as well to distinguish them:

> ("DNA Profiling," <u>The Encyclopedic
> Dictionary of Psychology</u>, 1983)

("DNA Profiling," The Encyclopedia of

Psychology, 1984).

If you have two authors with the same last name, use first initials:

(M. Woodman, 1989) . . . (J. Woodman, 1981)

If you have two or more works by the same author published in the same year, identify them on the reference list with lowercase letters in parentheses: (a), (b). In the text, use the following format:

(Zurer, 1992a) . . . (Zurer, 1992b)

If you wish to cite several articles within the same parentheses, arrange the authors' names alphabetically and use a semicolon to separate the entries:

Several studies (Carlisle, 1990; Lewin,

1992; Lowrie & Wells, 1991; Webb, 1992) show the

importance of DNA profiling to law enforcement

agencies.

For personal correspondence, letters, memos, lecture notes, e-mail, electronic bulletin boards, and so on, list only in the text itself, but not on the references page. Provide initials, surname of correspondent, plus the type of correspondence and date.

J. P. Miller (letter to author, April, 1989)

The Reference List in APA Style

The reference list, at the end of the research paper, contains all the sources actually used in the paper. When you use this documentation style, it is titled "References" or "Works Cited." The purpose of the reference list is to help readers find the materials you used in writing your paper. You must give complete and accurate information so that others may find the works. The following principles are generally accepted in documenting social science works, although many social science journals and fields have their own particular method of documenting. These guidelines have been adopted by the American Psychological Association (APA) in their style manual:

1. Present the author's surname and initials, followed by the date (in parentheses), the title, and the publication information.
2. The publication information required is place and name of publisher and date for books; date, volume and issue number, and page numbers for articles.
3. Place periods after the three main divisions: author, title, and publication information. Within these divisions, use commas to separate information.
4. Use capital letters for the first word only of a book or article title or following a colon in a subtitle. [For names of journals, capitalize all first letters.]
5. Underline titles of books, journals, magazines, and newspapers. Also underline volume numbers in journal references to indicate italics.

The accompanying model references and the term paper that follows both use the APA documentation format (and a few of the models) as found in the 1994 edition of *The Publication Manual of the American Psychological Association*. For additional examples and further information on documentation in the social sciences, consult the APA manual.

MODEL REFERENCES: SOCIAL SCIENCE (APA)

Type of Reference

BOOKS

1. One author

   ```
   Torrey, F. (1983). Surviving schizophrenia. New
        York: Harper & Row.
   ```

2. Two or more authors

   ```
   Minuchin, S., Rosman, B., & Baker, L. (1978).
        Psychosomatic families: Anorexia nervosa in
        context. Cambridge, MA: Harvard University
        Press.
   ```

3. Two or more books by the same author

   ```
   Bruch, H. (1973). Eating disorders: Obesity,
        anorexia nervosa, and the person within. New
        York: Basic Books.
   ```

Bruch, H. (1978). <u>The golden cage: The enigma of anorexia nervosa</u>. Cambridge, MA: Harvard University Press.

[Note: References are in chronological order.]

4. Book with editor(s)

Hartman, F. (Ed.). (1973). <u>World in crisis: Readings in international relations</u> (4th ed.). New York: Macmillan.

5. Essay, chapter, or section of an edited work

Cherns, A. (1982). Social research and its diffusion. In B. Appleby (Ed.), <u>Papers on social science utilisation</u> (pp. 316-326). Loughborough University of Technology: Centre for Utilisation of Social Science Research.

6. Encyclopedia entry

(signed)

Davidoff, L. (1984). Childhood psychosis. In the <u>Encyclopedia of psychology</u> (Vol. 10, pp. 156-157). New York: J. Wiley & Sons.

(unsigned)

Schizophrenia. (1983). In <u>The encyclopedic dictionary of psychology</u> (Vol. 8, pp. 501-502). Cambridge, MA: MIT Press.

7. Corporate author

American Psychiatric Association. (1980). <u>Diagnostic and statistical manual of mental disorders</u> (3d ed.). Washington, DC: Author.

[Note: The word *Author* here indicates that the author and publisher are the same.]

ARTICLES

1. Journal article (one author)

   Allen, J. (1985). Development of schizophrenia. Menninger Perspective, 2, 8-11.

2. Journal article (two authors)

   Steinhausen, H., & Glenville, K. (1983). Follow-up studies of anorexia nervosa: A review of research findings. Psychological Medicine, 13(2), 239-245.

3. Journal article (several authors)

   Garfinkle, P., Garner, D., Schwartz, D., & Thompson, M. (1980). Cultural expectations of thinness in women. Psychological Reports, 13, 483-491.

4. Magazine article (discontinuous pages, monthly)

   Miller, G. (1969, December). On turning psychology over to the unwashed. Psychology Today, pp. 53-54, 66-74.

5. Magazine article (no known author, weekly)

   The blood business. (1972, September 7). Time, pp. 47-48.

6. Newspaper article

   Eight APA journals initiate controversial blind reviewing. (1972, June). APA Monitor, p. 1.

7. Newspaper article (discontinuous pages)

Lublin, J. S. (1980, December 5). On idle: The
  unemployed shun much mundane work, at least
  for awhile. The Wall Street Journal,
  pp. A1, A25.

TECHNICAL REPORTS
1. Individual author

Gottfredson, L. S. (1980). How valid are
  occupational reinforcer pattern scores?
  (Report No. CSOS-R-292). Baltimore, MD:
  Johns Hopkins University, Center for Social
  Organization of Schools (ERIC Document
  Reproduction Service No. ED 182 465).

2. Corporate author

Life Insurance Marketing and Research Association.
  (1978). Profit and the AIB in United States
  ordinary companies (Research Rep.
  No. 1978-6). Hartford, CT: Author.

3. Government document

National Institute of Mental Health. (1982).
  Television and behavior: Ten years of
  scientific progress and implications in the
  eighties (DHHS Publication No. ADM 821195).
  Washington, DC: U.S. Government Printing
  Office.

OTHER SOURCES
1. Film or videotape

Maas, J. B. (Producer), & Gluck, D. H.
  (Director). (1979). Deeper into hypnosis
  [Film]. Englewood Cliffs, NJ: Prentice-Hall.

2. Abstracted or unpublished dissertation or thesis (in <u>Dissertation Abstracts</u>)

> Foster-Havercamp, M. E. (1982). An analysis of
> the relationship between preservice teacher
> training and directed teacher performance
> (Doctoral dissertation, University of
> Chicago, 1981). <u>Dissertation Abstracts</u>
> <u>International</u>, <u>42</u>, 4409A.

> Pendar, J. E. (1982). Undergraduate psychology
> majors: Factors influencing decision
> about college, curriculum and career.
> <u>Dissertation Abstracts International</u>, <u>42</u>,
> 4370A-4371A. (University Microfilms
> No. 82-06, 181)

3. Unpublished manuscript

> Cameron, S. E. (1981). <u>Educational level as a</u>
> <u>predictor of success</u>. Unpublished
> manuscript.

[Note: You can cite university affiliation for such works.]

4. Unpublished data

> Locke, C. (1983). [Survey of college women at
> Texas Tech University]. Unpublished raw
> data.

5. Review of book or film

> Carmody, T. P. (1982). A new look at medicine
> from the social perspective [Review of film
> <u>Social contexts of health, illness, and</u>
> <u>patient care</u>]. <u>Contemporary Psychology</u>, <u>27</u>,
> 208-209.

6. Interview
(*published*)

Newman, P. (1982, January). [Interview with
William Epstein, editor of JEP: Human
Perception and Performance]. APA Monitor,
pp. 7, 39.

(*unpublished*)

Hult, C. (1984, March). [Interview with Dr.
Lauro Cavazos, President, Texas Tech
University].

7. Personal correspondence
Do not list on reference page.

8. Paper presented at conference

Brewer, J. (1979, October). Energy, information,
and the control of heart rate. Paper
presented at the Society for Psycho-
physiological Research, Cincinnati, OH.

9. Television program

Miller, R. (Producer). (1982, May 21). Problems
of freedom. New York: NBC-TV.

10. Electronic information:

Online abstract:

Meyer, A. S., & Boch, K. (1992). The tip-of-the-
tongue phenomenon: Blocking or partial
activation? [Online]. Memory & Cognition,
20, 715-716. Abstract from: DIALOG File:
PsychINFO Item: 80-16351

CD-ROM abstract:

Meyer, A. S., & Boch, K. (1992). The tip-of-the-
tongue phenomenon: Blocking or partial
activation? [CD-ROM]. <u>Memory & Cognition</u>,
<u>20</u>, 715-716. Abstract from: SilverPlatter
File: PsychLIT Item: 80-16351

Online journal article:

Herz, J. C. (1995, April). Surfing on the
internet: A nethead's adventures online.
[Online serial]. Urban Desires, 1.3.
Available Internet: www/desires.com/ud.html.

Electronic Correspondence, such as e-mail messages and conversations via bulletin boards and electronic discussion groups are typically cited as personal communication in the text. In-text information to include:

author, date, subject of message;
name of the listserv, bulletin board, or e-mail discussion group available from: e-mail address.

[See also Li, X., & Crane, N. B. (1993). <u>A guide to citing electronic information</u>. Westport: Meckler.]

EXERCISES AND RESEARCH PROJECT

Follow the procedures outlined in this chapter to research a limited social science topic and write a social science research paper. The four exercises that follow give you additional practice in skills associated with research projects.

1. For each entry on your research paper bibliography, write a three- or four-sentence annotation describing the contents of that source.

2. Write a "review of the literature" report that summarizes in three to four pages the major ideas found in your sources. Often, a literature review, which lists and comments on the works done to date in a particular area, will be a component of a larger social science paper.

3. Write a report that details a primary research project and summarizes your findings. Use tables or graphs where possible to illustrate your results.

4. After you have completed your research paper, write an abstract of about 100 words that succinctly summarizes what your paper is about. An abstract should accurately reflect the scope and organization of your paper.

SAMPLE RESEARCH PAPER:
SOCIAL SCIENCE FORMAT (APA)

DNA Profiling:

The Scientific Equivalent

to Sherlock Holmes

Kirstin M. Roundy

Research Paper

Criminology 325

Professor James Miller

November 19, 1992

DNA Profiling 2

Abstract

This paper investigates the subject of DNA profiling; by discussing the DNA components and detailing the processes involved with developing a genetic fingerprint, the reader will gain a general understanding of DNA profiling and the effects it has had on criminology.

DNA Profiling 3

DNA Profiling: The Scientific Equivalent
to Sherlock Holmes

In a bulletin, "Crime in the United
States 1987," the Federal Bureau of
Investigations stated that over 1.3 million violent crimes were reported in the
United States during that year (Kirby,
1990, p. 4). This inconceivable number
includes approximately 90,000 rapes,
20,000 homicides, and 700,000 aggravated
assaults. When broken down into smaller,
more comprehensible numbers, these totals
are equivalent to one rape being commit-
ted every 4 to 5 minutes and a homicide
occurring every half hour. Even more
frightening than these statistics is the
fact that of the total violent crime
cases investigated, 60% of all reported
rapes and one quarter of all homicides
remain unsolved. Until recently, there
seemed to be little that society could do
to alleviate this problem.

DNA Fingerprinting

Background

In 1985, Dr. Alec Jeffreys devised a
method that promised to allow the court

DNA Profiling 4

system to convict or exonerate a suspect
based on a comparison of genetic information. This process, labeled as DNA
profiling, provided the court system with
a means of recognizing the guilty person,
and a way to make sure that the criminal,
not an innocent person, was punished for
the crime. DNA profiling, or fingerprinting as it is commonly known, has had a
vast and powerful effect on many aspects
of science. Therefore, it is the purpose
of this paper to further investigate the
subject of DNA profiling. By discussing
the DNA components and detailing the
processes involved with developing a
genetic fingerprint, the reader will gain
a general understanding of DNA profiling
and the effects it has had on forensic
science.

Although the human genome, the total
genetic makeup for a person, has been
studied for many years, it wasn't until
the 1900s that scientists began to fully
comprehend the function of the DNA molecule and its role in determining
heredity. During these years of discovery, scientists were able to determine

DNA Profiling 5

many of the specific details concerning the molecule, such as its structure, elemental makeup, and function. For, as the scientists discovered, DNA contains the exact blueprint for life. Every structure and function of the human body would not exist without the information found in this molecule. They also discovered that this molecule exists in the form of parallel strands that spiral around each other. These long strands, when combined with other proteins, become a tightly-packed, compact unit or chromosome (Raven and Johnson, 1989).

Chromosomes, existing as 23 pairs or 46 single units, are the distinguishable elements of heredity that are found in the nucleus. During conception, an individual will inherit half of the mother's and half of the father's chromosomes. This process helps to ensure that the individual's genome, with the exception of identical twins, will be genetically different from any other person's. This characteristic of inheritance makes DNA an appropriate molecule for use in identifying a suspect. If

guilty, the suspect's DNA pattern will
be the only one to match the DNA pattern
of evidence found at the scene of the
crime. Scientists also determined that
every cell with a nucleus contains DNA
in chromosomal form. After conception,
the cells of an individual undergo several thousand divisions during the
growth process. Since every new cell was
a result of division from the original
cell, each cell also contains the same
DNA. This fact is another reason that
makes DNA applicable for use in identification: the division process ensures
that the DNA found in one sample will be
the same for the whole organism. Similarly, as scientists were investigating
the basic purpose of DNA, they also discovered information pertaining to the
molecule's structure. Each DNA strand is
composed of a sequence of nucleotides,
which are each a combination of a sugar,
a phosphate group, and a nitrogen-con-
taining base (Raven and Johnson, 1989,
p. 284). When paired together, these
nucleotides spell out the genetic code
of an individual. The four nucleotides,

DNA Profiling 7

adenine, cytosine, guanine, and thymine,
line up in order along a single strand.
The DNA molecule is complete when the
nucleotides of single strand A pair up
with the nucleotides of single strand B.
The adenine nucleotide will always bond
with an opposite thymine while cytosine
will bond across with a guanine
nucleotide. Thus, the two strands
are bonded together to form the DNA molecule.

During their experimentation, scientists also discovered that it was the
various combinations of nucleotides that
actually made up a gene, the basic unit
of heredity. The sequence for a gene can
contain anywhere from 1000 to over 2 million individual nucleotides, while the
total human genome is believed to contain
50,000 to 100,000 genes. Each gene
assumes a specific position, or locus, on
a chromosome. When examining a pair of
chromosomes, the same gene can be found
at the same locus on each chromosome.
However, the genes may or may not be
exactly the same on each chromosome,
depending on which allele, an alternative

form of the gene, is inherited (Raven and Johnson, 1989).

Although genes make up a major part of DNA, there is another region, that which separates the individual genes, that is of equal importance. This region of separation, totaling 20% to 30% of the DNA in the genome (Tate, Mittleman, Donoghue, Jones, 1991, p. 20) does not appear to code for any particular function. As a result of this unusual characteristic, no scientist today can precisely explain this region's purpose for existence. However, it was these noncoding areas of the chromosome that led Dr. Alec Jeffreys to develop the process of DNA profiling.

In 1985, Jeffreys was studying a gene for myoglobin, a protein that stores oxygen in muscles. During his experimentation, he discovered one of the noncoding regions that exist between each gene; his region contained an unusual sequence of bases that were organized into a random number of repeat codes (Lowrie and Wells, 1991, p. 1). Jeffreys believed that these variable sequences

DNA Profiling 9

might be able to act as genetic markers, capable of tracking down a random gene and isolating its location on a chromosome. By extracting a specific repeat sequence and attaching it to a radioactive isotope, he was able to produce genetic probes that would bind to and reveal the location of other repeat sequences in a DNA sample.

Jeffreys' experiments also led him to the knowledge that these repeat sequences occurred in several areas of an individual's DNA, not just the myoglobin gene. The pattern of these sequences differs in each individual by the number of times each sequence is repeated. By analyzing an individual's sequence, a scientist can determine if an unknown sample came from this individual or another person by comparing the repeat sequences in both samples. This discovery became the basis for DNA profiling.

<u>The DNA Fingerprinting Process</u>

Even though Jeffreys' discovery was a new one, the processes he used to obtain the information were already

DNA Profiling 10

known. Obtaining a record of these highly
variable sequences, or, simply, a genetic
fingerprint, requires several steps. The
first step of the process involves the
extraction and isolation of DNA from a
sample. After the DNA is isolated from
the sample, restrictive enzymes are added
to the extracted DNA. These enzymes, chosen to recognize a certain base sequence,
act as molecular scissors and cut the DNA
chain into a series of fragments. The DNA
fragments are then placed in a culture
medium and are separated by a process
known as electrophoresis (Kirby, 1990).

Electrophoresis involves the running
of an electric current through the culture
medium, thus providing the fragments of
DNA with a negative charge. The charged
fragments, due to the laws of magnetic
attraction and repulsion, travel towards
the positive electrode. In a progressive
fashion, with the shorter fragments moving
quickly and the longer fragments moving
more slowly, the DNA fragments become separated by size. The culture medium is
then covered with a nylon membrane and a
layer of paper towels. This process, known

DNA Profiling 11

as Southern blotting, allows the
absorbency of the paper towels to act
upon the medium and, through capillary
action, draw the fragments of DNA up into
the nylon membrane (Kirby, 1990).

At this point, the DNA fragments are
denatured, separated from their double
helix into a single strand form. The
nylon membrane is then immersed into a
solution of radioactive probes. These
probes will mix with the denatured fragments of DNA and bond to any
complementary variable sequences found in
the membrane. The final step of the
process involves making the pattern of
bonded variable sequences visible. This
goal is achieved by placing an x-ray film
next to the membrane. The radioactive
probes emit radiation, thus exposing the
film and causing a foggy band to appear
on the surface. The resulting pattern of
bands is the DNA fingerprint. The
autorad, or developed x-ray film, is then
read manually by an analyst. By comparing
the bands of this sample with another
one, the analyst can determine if the
organisms are related or not. These

DNA Profiling 12

interpretations and conclusions complete
the fingerprinting process (Kirby, 1990).

Applications of DNA Information

Although the idea of DNA profiling
was discovered by experimentation with
the myoglobin gene, its present-day
applications exceed its original purposes. Today, genetic fingerprinting has
expanded into several aspects of the life
sciences (Franklin-Barbajosa, p. 112). In
the area of zoology, fingerprinting has
been used to further understand the
breeding patterns of wild animals. For
those animals in captivity, this process
also allows zoologists to identify unre-
lated animal pairs for desired traits to
increase the genetic diversity of the
species. Doctors utilize fingerprinting
to determine the success of a bone marrow
transplant in a chemotherapy patient. A
successful transplant will be indicated
if the donor's fingerprint bands appear
in a DNA sample of the patient's blood.
Two of the most familiar applications of
DNA fingerprinting involve the solving of
paternity cases and identifying a suspect

DNA Profiling 13

in a violent crime case. It is with this last application, in the area of forensic science, that DNA fingerprinting has gained its public acclaim.

As DNA fingerprinting is closely tied to the life sciences, forensic science also maintains a close proximity to other fields. Its association is further explained in this quote: "Forensic science involves the application of many scientific expertises (biology, chemistry, toxicology, medicine) to situations concerned with courts of justice or public debate" (Office of Technology Assessment, 1990, p. 40). The field of forensics involves the application of given evidence and acquired knowledge to a specific court case. To a forensic scientist, DNA profiling is "the greatest advance in crime-fighting technology since fingerprints" (Thompson and Ford, 1990, p. 38). DNA fingerprinting allows the forensic scientist to obtain a means of identification of the criminal from minute pieces of biological evidence.

For several years prior to the invention of DNA profiling, forensic ana-

DNA Profiling 14

lyst used various genetic markers to
analyze biological evidence. However,
these methods were only able to exclude
certain individuals from a list of suspects; they could not accurately describe
who the criminal actually was. For
instance, if a blood stain found at the
crime scene contained the same red blood
cell antigens as the suspect, an analyst
would only be able to report that the
suspect *may* have been responsible for the
blood stain. Due to the commonalities of
blood cell antigens in a population, a
larger percentage of individuals could
have the same antigen (Thornton, 1989,
p. 18). These methods were inconclusive
and provided little information about
possible suspects.

    With DNA profiling, the information
gained from a DNA analysis of a biological sample, when compared with other
samples, decisively determines the identity of the criminal. By using DNA
fingerprinting to analyze evidence,
forensic scientists can use various
sources of biological evidence, such as
blood, semen, and hair, to obtain a sam-

DNA Profiling 15

ple of DNA for identification. In many of the violent crime cases, these biological samples are the only evidence available.

Controversies of DNA Fingerprinting

Since its "debut" in 1985, DNA pro-filing has been used to solve hundreds of murder, rape, and paternity cases through-out the United States and England. The Narborough Murder Inquiry was the first murder investigation to utilize DNA fin-gerprinting. This case involved the rape and murder of two 15-year-old girls over the space of three years. A DNA analysis of semen and stain material indicated that the same person had killed both girls. A 17-year-old boy, who had signed a confes-sion stating that he had killed both girls, was charged with the murders. How-ever, analysis of his DNA proved that he was not the killer. This boy was the first suspect to be exonerated of a crime by the results of DNA fingerprinting. The real murderer was finally identified and sentenced in January 1988 (McCabe, 1992, p. 540; Wambaugh, 1989).

This case thoroughly proved the capabilities of DNA profiling in identifying and exonerating suspects. It was through the Narborough Murder Inquiry that DNA fingerprinting gained publicity in the United States. The enthusiasm was so great that, within two years, three private companies were offering DNA analysis services. Even the FBI became entangled in the excitement and began investigations into implementing its own program. Basically, the idea of DNA fingerprinting was fully embraced by the United States. At first, few scientists would refute its methods, and the courts never challenged its use as evidence. No one doubted the power of DNA profiling.

However, in 1989, scientists began to question the accuracy and reliability of DNA tests. Many people believed that, due to the rush to implement DNA profiling in this country, several necessary rules and requirements were overlooked. Since each of the companies had formed on its own, there was no standard list of procedures for the process of fingerprinting; each company conducted the

DNA Profiling 17

analysis in their own way. There was also
no committee set up to regulate the company's proceedings. Basically, the
American public naively accepted DNA profiling without knowing much about it.
However, the largest problem arose with
the courts. In the first years of DNA
fingerprinting use in the United States,
the court system had blindly accepted DNA
analysis as evidence. Then, the courts
began to reconsider the admissibility of
DNA profiling as evidence.

In the United States, to be considered as scientific evidence, any
scientific technique must pass the Frye
test. A 1923 ruling, the Frye test
requires that the technique be generally
accepted in the scientific community to
which it belongs before it can be used as
scientific evidence (Office of Technology
Assessment, 1990, p. 91). Since many scientists had begun to debate the
reliability of DNA profiling, it was,
obviously, not wholly accepted in the
scientific community. In August 1989, a
New York judge ruled that a DNA test,
performed by a private company, could not

DNA Profiling 18

be used as evidence in a murder case
(Thompson and Ford, 1990, p. 38). This
unprecedented ruling provoked several
judges across the nation to make the same
decision regarding DNA profiling evidence. It also convinced many people that
even the most believable scientific techniques can be misused or analyzed
incorrectly.

Conclusion

By discussing the various aspects of
DNA profiling, it is clear to see why
this process has had such a powerful
effect on the science community. In the
different areas of science where the technique was applicable, profiling has
revolutionized the way in which experiments are performed. However, since 1989,
little has changed regarding the treatment
of DNA profiling. Various committees have
been formed, but regulations and standards
for the process are still unclear.

Many people still believe in the
process while others continue to have
doubts. However, as Victor McKusick

DNA Profiling 19

states, regardless of the possible mistakes involved with DNA fingerprinting,
the benefits of this miraculous process
far outweigh any negative aspects: "When
performed properly, the technique is
capable of providing strong evidence for
solving crimes. We think it is a powerful
tool for criminal investigations and for
the exoneration of innocent individuals,
and on that basis should continue to be
used. . . ." (McKusick as quoted in
Zurer, 1992b, p. 4).

DNA Profiling 20

References

Brown, P. (1991). "Foolproof" DNA fingerprints within grasp. New Scientist,
132, 14.

Carlile, A. (1990). Science in court.
Chemistry & Industry, 18, 580.

Charles, D. (1991). Convicts' DNA prints
added to US police files. New Scientist, 131, 19-20.

Charles, D. (1992). Courtroom battles
over genetic fingerprinting. New
Scientist, 134, 10.

Coghlan, A., and Joyce, C. (1989). Public
debate grows over genetic fingerprinting. New Scientist, 124, 1686.

Ezzell, C. (1992). Panel oks DNA fingerprints in court cases. Science News,
144, 261-268.

Franklin-Barbajosa, C. (1992). DNA profiling: The new science of identity.
National Geographic, 101, 112-116.

Kirby, L. (1990). DNA fingerprinting: An
introduction. New York: Stockton
Press.

Lewin, R. (1992). Matching of DNA fingerprints prompts renewed concern. New
Scientist, 133, 13.

DNA Profiling 21

Long, J. (1988). Admissibility of DNA
    test results evidence debated. Chem-
    ical & Engineering News, 66, 19-21.

Lowrie, P., and Wells, S. (1991). Genetic
    fingerprinting. New Scientist, 131,
    1-4.

McCabe, E. (1992). Applications of DNA
    fingerprinting in pediatric prac-
    tice. The Journal of Pediatrics,
    120, 499-509.

National Research Council. (1992). DNA
    technology in forensic science.
    Washington, D.C.: National Academy
    Press.

Nichols, R., and Balding, D. (1991).
    Effects of population structure on
    DNA fingerprint. Heredity, 66,
    297-302.

Office of Technology Assessment, Congress
    of the United States. (1990, July).
    Genetic witness: Forensic uses of
    DNA tests.

Raven, P., and Johnson, G. (1989). Biol-
    ogy, 2nd ed. St Louis, MO: Times
    Mirror/Mosby College Publishing.

Tate, L., Mittleman, R., Donoghue, E.,
    and Jones, A. (1991). Forensic

DNA Profiling 22

pathology in the 1980s. American
Journal of Clinical Pathology, 96,
S20-S24.

Thompson, W., and Ford, S. (1990). Is DNA
fingerprinting ready for the courts.
New Scientist, 125, 38-43.

Thornton, J. (1989). DNA profiling: New
tool links evidence to suspects with
high certainty. Chemical & Engineering News, 67, 18-27.

United States Senate. (1989, March).
Genetic testing as a means of criminal investigation. Hearing before
the subcommittee on the Constitution
of the Committee on the Judiciary.
One hundred first Congress, first
session. Available from: U.S. Government Printing Office. Washington,
DC:#J-101-4.

Vogel, S. (1990). The case of the unrav-
eling DNA. Discover, 11, 46-47.

Wambaugh, J. (1989). The blooding. New
York: William Morrow and Company,
Inc.

Webb, J. (1992). Police attacked over DNA
fingerprinting. New Scientist, 133,
12.

DNA Profiling 23

Weisburd, S. (1988). Fingerprinting DNA
    from a single hair. Science News,
    133, 262-263.

Weiss, R. (1989). DNA takes the stand.
    Science News, 136, 74-76.

Zurer, P. (1989). DNA profiling on trial-
    judge bars unreliable results.
    Chemical & Engineering News, 67,
    6-7.

Zurer, P. (1990). DNA fingerprinting
    standards needed. Chemical & Engi-
    neering News, 68, 6.

Zurer, P. (1992a). FBI director defends
    use of DNA profiling. Chemical &
    Engineering News, 70, 7-8.

Zurer, P. (1992b). DNA fingerprinting:
    Use upheld but strict standards
    urged. Chemical & Engineering News,
    70, 4-5.

Index

✦ ✦ ✦

The abbreviation f stands for figure